Wanda E. Brunstetter's

Amish Friends Farm-to-Table Cookbook

280 Amazing Recipes Help Encourage Local Farming Networks

BARBOUR PUBLISHING

Print ISBN 979-8-89151-097-5

Compiled by Rebecca Germany.

Top cover photo: Doyle Yoder Photography.

Published by Barbour Publishing, Inc., 1810 Barbour Drive, Uhrichsville, Ohio 44683, www.barbourbooks.com

Our mission is to inspire the world with the life-changing message of the Bible.

Member of the Evangelical Christian Publishers Association

Printed in China.

Introduction

My husband and I are blessed to have many Amish friends in several communities. We have eaten meals in their homes on numerous occasions. A good deal of those meals included foods grown in their own gardens or from local farms and produce stands. It allows you to appreciate the amount of time and effort it takes to grow and harvest fresh produce and how it provides for so many people.

Cooking farm fresh ingredients is a healthy choice. Fresh produce is more nutrient dense than anything you find at a grocery store. Locally grown food is harvested at the peak of ripeness and arrives at your table immediately. A product's nutritional content decreases through air exposure, artificial lighting, and temperature changes. Local food avoids all of these because of its short or nonexistent travel. Eating food from farm to table can have many health benefits, especially if it's organically grown. When you prepare your own food, you also control how much sugar, salt, and fat goes into it. Meals prepared at home typically have fewer calories than meals from restaurants or ordering takeout. There's nothing like eating a tossed salad made with fresh produce from one's own garden.

I hope you will appreciate the variety of tasty meals in this cookbook that my Amish friends have shared, featuring food from farms to their tables. I'm sure it'll bring Amish cuisine authenticity to your taste buds.

I wish to thank my editor, Rebecca Germany, for taking the time to see that the recipes submitted by Amish friends were compiled in this special farm-to-table cookbook.

Wanda E. Brunstetter

Contents

Therefore be patient, brethren, until the coming of the Lord. See how the farmer waits for the precious fruit of the earth, waiting patiently for it until it receives the early and latter rain.

—James 5:7 NKJV

APPLY

What difference does it make in your life that Jesus is your good shepherd?

What does it mean to you that the good shepherd knows you as His sheep?

PRAY

DATE:..

SHARE WHAT YOU HAVE RECEIVED FROM GOD

READ 1 PETER 4:1–11

UNDERSTAND

The grace of God is a gift you have been given, but Peter knew that there's a good deal of work and intention that goes into fully enjoying and sharing that gift from the Lord. Prayer requires discipline in order to keep it a top priority, and love calls for perseverance when those around you are engaged in sin. Hospitality will be inconvenient, but it has long been a way to honor others and to care for their needs.

By calling God's people "stewards" of God's grace, Peter was making a point that grace isn't just for us to keep for ourselves but a gift we should share readily. You have been blessed because God sees the potential in you to carry His influence to others. He sees the potential in you for love, generosity, and peace. When you care for others, you release to them the kindness that God has already given to you.

Your invitation from God today is to find new ways to bless others with the love and mercy He has given you. And wonderfully, along the way, you'll find people who offer that same love and mercy back to you.

....

....

....

....

....

....

....

APPLY

Why did Peter place love above all else?

How did Peter say you should use the gifts God has given you?

PRAY

DATE: ....

COSTLY TRUST

READ PSALM 139:19–24

UNDERSTAND

God's most disquieting actions happen because He is holy: His judgment, wrath, jealousy, and even vengeance. His other characteristics are much more comforting: His love, grace, mercy, and faithfulness.

Yet holiness is the attribute of God mentioned most often in the Bible. And, as 1 Peter 1:16 (NKJV) points out, He calls us to be holy: "Be holy, for I am holy." Holiness matters, but how do we practice it?

Like David in Psalm 139, we need to focus on a right relationship with God. Christ makes that possible. In practice, holiness means we love what God loves and hate what He hates—not in a judgmental way, thinking ourselves superior, but understanding that sin has corrupted God's good creation and that we are desperate for Him to make things right.

He makes things right through Jesus. Christ in us makes us holy, set apart by God for God's purposes and pleasure. Our obedience demonstrates our desire to be holy like He is holy. As we do this, we join with David, who wrapped up Psalm 139 by opening himself up to divine scrutiny: "Search me, O God, and know my heart" (verse 23 NKJV). Where David obeyed in anticipation, we obey in response to Jesus' finished work. And in that obedience, we are His holiness in action.

....

....

....

....

....

....

APPLY

What comes to mind when you think of God's holiness?

What are the challenges of asking God to show you how you can improve in holiness?

PRAY

DATE: ....

BELIEVING IS SEEING

READ HEBREWS 11:1–6

UNDERSTAND

The pursuit of God is sometimes made more challenging by the fact that we can't see Him. It's so much easier to believe in what we can perceive with our senses, even though we know they are limited. But if faith was based only on what we could perceive, it would be science, not faith. And even science has its limits.

God's interactions with us give faith an anchor in history. He made Himself known to people from the beginning and then made Himself visible in Jesus Christ. Even though we don't see the Holy Spirit enter us when we're saved, the proof of His presence is in the way He changes us. Hebrews 11:1 (NIV) says, "Faith is confidence in what we hope for and assurance about what we do not see." When we take that to heart, we don't stay the same. God teaches us to live in light of a greater world. Hebrews 11:16 (NIV) says we long for the reward of "a better country—a heavenly one."

Don't underestimate the anchoring power of that promised reward for the faithful. Believe that everything you go through now is worth it, that God sees you and will reward you for sticking with Him no matter what. Believing is seeing. Believe it now, when your flesh still clouds your eyes, and one day you will see Him face-to-face.

....

....

....

....

....

....

APPLY

What are some of God's attributes that you've witnessed in your life?

What are the challenges of pursuing an invisible God?

PRAY

DATE: ....

CELEBRATE GENEROUS GRACE FOR OTHERS

READ MATTHEW 20:1–16

UNDERSTAND

The workers in the vineyard who showed up late needed to receive a full wage in order to feed their families. While it would have technically been just for the vineyard owner to pay them only for the time they worked, such a small payment would not have been very compassionate or in touch with their actual needs. Yet, the generosity they received became a point of division with their fellow workers. Seeing mercy and grace shown to others sometimes becomes a source of contention.

God sees how humanity has failed and is more than willing to treat people far better than they deserve. That may sound like really great news for you personally, but once you see someone else get the same kind of mercy, you may have a very different view of God. Is God merely giving others a free pass for their sins? Don't the commands of God matter?

Obedience does matter a great deal to God, but so do mercy and restoration. There isn't a limited supply of God's grace. In fact, everyone is treated with more grace than they deserve before God. Jesus doesn't want you to resent anyone else's need for mercy, because we're *all* in need, and without God's grace we'd have nowhere to go.

....

....

....

....

....

APPLY

Why does Jesus say the first will be last and the last will be first in God's kingdom?

How does God's generosity run counter to the expectations of society today?

PRAY

DATE: ....

UNDERSTANDING LEADS TO FRUITFULNESS

READ MATTHEW 13:1–11, 16–23

UNDERSTAND

The words of Jesus have tremendous potential to change your life and the lives of others, but that change isn't going to happen without intentionality on your part. Life is filled with conflict and distractions. You can go off course easily, losing sight of God's wisdom and chasing after something that feels good today but fails you over the long term. Part of the problem for those distracted by the cares of this life is the lack of time given to reflection on Jesus' teachings.

Today you can consider what it looks like to truly understand what Jesus has to say to you. You can pause and dig deeper into your own life, asking questions or taking an inventory of your soul. What worries you? What do you desire? What are you seeking? There are plenty of ways to uncover what other than Jesus' words has taken root in your life.

Once you have an idea of the distractions and challenges you face, consider the ways you can help the words of Jesus take root in your life. How can you keep His message in front of you so that you won't wilt under adversity or toss His promises aside for the world's offerings?

The fruit of God's Word shows up gradually, but if you invest time today in understanding the message of Jesus, you'll find new growth springing forth in your life.

....

....

....

....

APPLY

What does it mean for someone who hears God's Word to be fruitful?

How do worries prevent disciples of Jesus from being fruitful?

PRAY

DATE: ....

WHERE ARE YOUR ROOTS?

READ COLOSSIANS 2:6–15

UNDERSTAND

Having a strong start with Jesus is a great thing, but the apostle Paul wrote about the importance of growing roots that go deep with Him. Paul wanted his readers to keep returning to the basics of the faith, such as loving God and living by faith. But he also wanted them to seek to go deeper by applying the teachings of Jesus to their lives and by learning to keep in touch with the Spirit.

It's easy for alternative belief systems to creep in and replace your roots in Christ. Whether that outside influence comes from a political system, a philosophy, or a cultural movement, your roots in Christ must be tended and cared for, while the harmful beliefs should be uprooted as soon as possible.

The idea of living your life in Christ may seem to be a vague concept. So how can you live "in" a God you can't see? It's most likely that Paul was referring to the orientation of a believer's heart, desires, and mind. He wanted us to keep Jesus at the forefront of how we live each day, remaining mindful of Him and desiring quiet intimacy with Him.

....

....

....

....

....

....

....

....

APPLY

What are the advantages of staying rooted in Jesus?

....

....

....

....

....

....

....

....

....

....

....

....

....

What is the role of thanksgiving in remaining rooted in Jesus?

....

....

....

....

....

....

....

....

....

....

....

....

PRAY

....

....

....

....

....

....

DATE: ....

ONE IN A HUNDRED

READ MATTHEW 18:12–14

UNDERSTAND

Getting spiritually lost looks similar to getting physically lost while driving. The Bible is your map, and the Holy Spirit is your divine GPS, but you still get off track. You thought you knew the way—how to pray, how to act humbly, how to lead yourself and your family—but then unfamiliar sights started showing up, followed by that nagging feeling that you're off course.

When the kids have gone haywire, or communication lines between you and your wife are down, or you're just not feeling like God is there, it's scary, and that fear can easily replace your confidence in God's sovereign care. So, you try to course-correct based on your own thoughts and get even more lost.

Whether you get physically lost driving or go spiritually astray, pride is often the biggest obstacle to getting back on track. God knows when you're lost. He also knows how to find you. Whatever may be keeping you from asking for help, your good shepherd is still coming to find you. Stop trying to fix it, hide, or act like you're okay. Stand still and call out. You may be the one in a hundred He is looking for.

....

....

....

....

....

....

....

APPLY

What do you do when you realize you're lost—keep going or seek directions?

How quick are you to pray when things aren't going well?

PRAY

DATE: ....

FREEDOM REQUIRES SACRIFICE

READ 1 KINGS 22:1–8, 26–28, 30–36

UNDERSTAND

Seeking what God has to say before you act is great advice, but in today's passage, there's a lot more to chew on.

First, look at the history: Jehoshaphat was one of the rare God-honoring kings, so before he allied himself with King Ahab of Israel, he wanted to see what God had to say to them. In those days, to hear from God, you asked a prophet. Ahab knew that a true prophet would have only bad things to say to him. So he kept false prophets around: ear ticklers and sycophants. But real freedom means accepting difficult-to-hear truths. Inquiring first of God means being open to His redirection, trusting He knows best.

Next, listen to the right message: Jehoshaphat knew of one prophet, Micaiah, who would speak God's truth no matter the cost to himself. And when Micaiah did, Ahab ordered him to be jailed until he himself returned from battle. Micaiah's response showed his trust in God: If God had spoken through him, Ahab would die in battle; if God hadn't, he wouldn't. It was a simple test he staked his freedom on.

Finally, live in touch with reality: Ahab attempted to disguise himself in battle, but he still died of a seemingly random arrow wound. Since God's will is going to happen whether you're on board or not, why not get on board? Prepare for whatever the day may bring by seeking God first.

....

....

....

....

APPLY

What does freedom look like to you?

What's your tendency with God: to ask for permission or forgiveness?

PRAY

DATE: ....

HOPE IN GOD ALONE

READ PSALM 71:1–12

UNDERSTAND

The psalms often use images of conflict and battle to describe the threats and challenges of life that oppose the security found in God. But you don't have to be facing a personal enemy or a difficult relationship in order to feel like you're in the midst of conflict and in need of God's security. The enemy could be a medical diagnosis or a traumatic experience that haunts your thoughts. In each case, you may face adversity that makes it more necessary than ever to rely on God.

There are plenty of places where you can seek refuge. In fact, your greatest temptation may be to rely on something other than God for protection in the midst of conflict, suffering, or uncertainty. That is where idolatry comes in, as you find yourself relying more on money, powerful relationships, or possessions for security. An idol is anything that replaces the role of God in your life and keeps you from intimacy with Him.

Seeing God as your security and hope for the future is a process. Today's psalm tells us about learning to trust in God from the days of one's youth. It's never too soon or too late to start trusting God with the challenges of your life. It's something you learn and cultivate over time. But soon it will become natural to turn to God first when your life is out of sorts and uncertain.

....

....

....

....

....

APPLY

What are some of the images used in Psalm 71 to describe God?

What does it mean to be rescued by God in your own circumstances today?

PRAY

DATE: ....

GETTING UNSTUCK

READ PROVERBS 8:17

UNDERSTAND

God knows you're busy. While you're beating yourself up because you can barely carve out five minutes a day to focus on Him, He loves that you're making time at all. After all, God can do more with five minutes than you can with a whole week.

Don't get stuck thinking that God is tapping His foot, arms folded, thinking you're a doofus because you spend too little time building your faith and too much time trying to fix things you can't control.

Instead, picture Him as your Father, waiting with open arms. He is there no matter what, willing and able to comfort, give wisdom, and show grace. He brings challenges sometimes, but everything He does is to help you learn, grow, and know Him better. If anything, He wishes you would call Him more often, let Him know how you're doing, and thank Him for being a good dad.

If you're stuck in a rut and just need someone who understands that, Jesus does. He got worn out and beaten up too—but He allowed it so He could identify with you in your hard times and give you that deep understanding your soul is dying for. Focus on Him and let Him help you get unstuck.

....

....

....

....

....

....

....

APPLY

What keeps you from spending as much time with God as you think you should?

....

....

....

....

....

....

....

....

....

....

....

....

Do you think God is frustrated with your absence or looking forward to your presence?

....

....

....

....

....

....

....

....

....

....

....

....

PRAY

....

....

....

....

....

....

DATE: ....

THE BIBLICAL HEROES HILKIAH AND EZRA

READ 2 KINGS 22:1–23:3

UNDERSTAND

Wicked King Manasseh reigned over Judah hundreds of years after Moses, David, and many of the other Old Testament writers. Manasseh considered nothing sacred. You could compare him to the wicked sorcerer in *Indiana Jones and the Temple of Doom*; but instead of sacrificing other people's children, he passed his own son through the fire (2 Kings 21:6)—as well as any copies of the scriptures he could find, it seems.

A generation later, not even the high priest in Jerusalem had a copy of God's Word, until the day Hilkiah the high priest exclaimed, "I have found the Book of the Law" (2 Kings 22:8 NIV). This occurred just before the Babylonian captivity of the nation of Israel in 386 BC.

Fortunately, the Israelites took the then-completed books of the Old Testament to Babylon and preserved them throughout their captivity. Hilkiah's family apparently retained the rediscovered scriptures and passed them down from generation to generation. It was Hilkiah's great-grandson Ezra who had a copy of the scriptures with him when he returned with the released captives to Jerusalem.

It's common to wonder, "Do we have all the right books in God's Word?" but thankfully, we can trust that God, who miraculously preserved the books of the Old Testament despite persecution and national apostasy, has kept His Word to us complete.

....

....

....

....

APPLY

Why do you think God preserved the Hebrew scriptures?

Does anyone need to wonder or worry about lost books of the Bible? Why?

PRAY

DATE: ....

QUICK TO FORGIVE

READ PSALM 32

UNDERSTAND

In Ephesians 4:32, Paul called us to forgive others to the extent that Jesus has forgiven us. Why, then, do we hang on to how we've been wronged or the wrongs we've done? Accident or not, the damage is real: We carry the wrongdoing as a physical weight, an emotional millstone. Surely God has more for His children.

And so He does. But it all begins with forgiveness—Him forgiving us. Our problems start when we think we don't have much that needs to be forgiven or we're undeserving of what's happened. We're better than most, aren't we? But Isaiah 64:6 (NLT) reminds us that all our righteous deeds "are nothing but filthy rags."

Psalm 7:11 (NKJV) says, "God is a just judge, and God is angry with the wicked every day." Our offense is always against Him first and foremost—and yet, He longs to forgive us. Jesus obeyed the Father's will so we could be forgiven. Forgiveness on our part isn't a matter of feeling, then, but obedience and a response to His forgiveness. Under grace, we must forgive.

Loving what God loves is learning to forgive, especially when someone doesn't deserve it. When you do that, you will find yourself, as David did, surrounded by mercy. Let God's forgiveness wash over you anew.

....

....

....

....

....

....

APPLY

What specific things has God forgiven you for?

....

....

....

....

....

....

....

....

....

....

....

....

....

How hard is it for you to forgive others? Why?

....

....

....

....

....

....

....

....

....

....

....

....

....

PRAY

....

....

....

....

....

....

DATE: ....

TRUST DESPITE CONFUSION

READ LUKE 2:41–52

UNDERSTAND

Imagine the thrill of horror that went through Joseph's and Mary's hearts as they realized they had left Jesus behind in the enormous crowds leaving Jerusalem.

When they finally found Jesus, His response was just plain confusing. We've all heard bizarre or infuriatingly patronizing things come from the mouths of twelve-year-olds (if only because we remember being twelve!), but this was an all-timer: "You should've known I'd be hanging out in My Father's house."

On the one hand, Mary and Joseph might have been expecting an apology: "Sorry I scared you, Mom and Dad." But then there is the whole reference to Jesus' Father, whom they knew didn't mean Joseph, which brought up everything that was so alien to them about this boy they had raised and loved.

Sometimes what God's Word says isn't clear; sometimes it is, but it cuts right to the core of an embarrassing habit. And yet, He knows best and cares the most, doesn't He? Part of pursuing God is learning to deal with that tension. When Jesus confuses you, remember that He always wants what's best for you, even when you can't see what He's doing. If you can trust Him at those key moments of uncertainty, fear, and desperate hope, He will not let you down.

....

....

....

....

....

....

APPLY

What about God is hardest for you to understand?

How difficult is it to trust God fully when you don't understand what He's doing?

PRAY

DATE: ....

THE HORIZON OF RECOVERY

READ DEUTERONOMY 4:26–31

UNDERSTAND

Deuteronomy 4:29 (NIV) says, "If from there you seek the LORD"—but where is there? At this point in Israel's history, God had delivered the first generation from Egypt after they'd blown it by constantly doubting Him and turning back to their familiar idols. After this latest fresh start, Moses predicted they would blow it again. That's where the *there* comes in: From that next point of sin and distress, they would call out to God.

Fortunately, there was (and is) good news: Deuteronomy 4:31 (NKJV) affirms that even when you blow it (again), God is right there; and when you turn from your sin and back to Him and His ways, "He will not forsake you nor destroy you, nor forget the covenant of your fathers which He swore to them." Bottom line: God is always faithful to keep His promises, to do what is right.

The trajectory of seeking God has some huge ups and downs. But He is the unchanging horizon that helps you reorient and look for Him again. When you make a habit of that—seeking Him and being willing to change based on what you learn—He will reward your faith by anchoring you to Himself.

....

....

....

....

....

....

....

APPLY

What are some ways you seek God?

How hard is it for you to turn back to God when you've strayed?

PRAY

DATE: ....

MERCY LEADS TO REPENTANCE

READ ACTS 3:17–26

UNDERSTAND

Humanly speaking, the apostle Peter had every reason to feel angry, even judgmental, toward the people who had either ignored Jesus' message or actively opposed Him. Yet, he stuck with Jesus' mission to bring repentance and renewal, not condemnation.

It's not easy to talk to an indifferent or hostile listener about Jesus, but that is exactly what Peter did in Acts 3. After healing a lame beggar at the temple, he spoke to a group of amazed onlookers, many of whom had probably approved of the crucifixion of Jesus weeks before. Peter's example shows that mercy can win out over judgment, as many of his listeners responded positively to his message.

God's kindness is well documented throughout scripture, and that kindness leads people to repent of their sins. Just as you have been forgiven by God, you can show the same forgiveness to others. In fact, Jesus expects just that.

It may feel good in the moment to condemn or judge others, but that won't lead to the refreshment God desires for the world. The Lord has given each of us a holy calling to show others the path to God. The hope is that their sins can be wiped away for times of refreshing, but sharing that message can be challenging. The grace of God can feel risky and costly, but when others respond to it, the effort is well worth it.

....

....

....

....

....

APPLY

What does repentance and "turning to God" look like in your life?

What is the promised result of repentance?

PRAY

DATE: ....

SPIRIT AND TRUTH

READ JOHN 4:23-26

UNDERSTAND

Jesus made an intriguing statement in John 4:24 in the middle of His discussion with the Samaritan woman at the well: God is looking for those who will worship Him in spirit and truth. Their talk had turned to worship. The Samaritans had Mount Gerizim, their own local place where they worshipped God, and the Jews had the temple in Jerusalem. This woman wanted to know which was the right place, but she was asking the wrong question.

The question isn't where but whom and how. That's what Jesus was getting at—to worship God in the way God approves is to consider twin factors: spirit and truth. There is only one who continually worships God in this committed, right-hearted way: Jesus Christ Himself. So, it is only because we are His that we can be true worshippers.

In worship, we should focus on what matters most to the Spirit—the glorification of Jesus Christ. Since Jesus Himself is the only true worshipper, our worship should focus on what means so much to Him: the good news of God's grace.

Anyone gathered in spirit and truth—disregarding barriers of class, gender, age, nationality, and ethnicity—is on track and ready to worship God the way He told us to: focusing on God's will and words and celebrating Him.

....

....

....

....

....

APPLY

What is your favorite way to worship God?

What distracts you from worshipping God with a full, right heart?

PRAY

DATE: ....

NOBODY'S LOOKING

READ PSALM 14

UNDERSTAND

Some of us are really good at sharing about Jesus. But a lot of us hold back; we're introverts or don't want to be rejected or worried about blowing our reputation ("Yeah, he's a Christian, but don't worry—he's cool").

Psalm 14 is a wake-up call to stop caring about cool. The world is full of cool people who want nothing to do with God. Some of them hate God and anyone who wants anything to do with Him. Even so, we must tell them about Jesus.

We each have our stories about how God changed us through the gospel. Your story doesn't have to be spectacular; God's Spirit will make the impact because He knows each person's heart and how to reach everyone. Our part is sharing the gospel. Romans 10:17 (NIV) says, "Faith comes from hearing the message."

Trust the power of the message. Psalm 14:5–6 (ESV) says that you are part of "the generation of the righteous" and that "the LORD is [your] refuge." When you represent Him to this broken world, He has your back, no matter its reaction. Nobody is looking for Him, but we weren't either until we heard about Jesus.

....

....

....

....

....

....

....

APPLY

How do you tend to view nonbelievers—as knuckle-heads or lost sheep?

Which describes your general view of God better—wrathful judge or open-armed father?

PRAY

DATE: ....

THE REWARDS OF PERSISTENT, HUMBLE PRAYER

READ MATTHEW 15:21–28

UNDERSTAND

Humility and prayer go hand in hand. When you approach God, it is essential to know your place before your Creator. While God's mercy and grace are abundant, there also is no guarantee that your prayer request and God's desires are going to match up. So if you approach prayer with a humble understanding that God is not obligated to grant your request, it's actually more likely that He will grant it.

The story about Jesus at first ignoring a Gentile woman's desperate plea for help can feel jarring. But her persistence in the face of what seems like rejection teaches us that we sometimes have to stick with it in our prayers, knowing that God won't ignore us but may be waiting to give us what we've asked for. There's no magic number of days to persist in prayer. It's possible that we may have to persist in prayer for years before God moves on our behalf.

As you humbly seek God and bring your requests to Him, you can rest in His goodness and compassion. He welcomes your persistent prayers. One day, though maybe not until you are in the glory of God's presence, you will see the rewards of your perseverance.

....

....

....

....

....

....

....

APPLY

In what areas of your life do you need Jesus to step in and help you?

....

....

....

....

....

....

....

....

....

....

....

....

What does Matthew 15:21–28 teach about persistent, humble prayer?

....

....

....

....

....

....

....

....

....

....

....

....

PRAY

....

....

....

....

....

....

DATE: ....

THE MISSION

READ HEBREWS 10:23-25

UNDERSTAND

God is all about relationship. The most harmonious, joyful relationship ever is shared among Father, Son, and Holy Spirit. So it makes sense that something special happens when God's people gather to worship Him and seek His face—that is, with no agenda other than to honor Him and deepen the relationship. Vital things happen in fellowship that can't happen when you're alone.

The church is Christ's body, all the parts working together to accomplish what He, as the head, wants. At church, He wakes us up spiritually, reminding us both of our separation *from* the world and of our shared mission *to* the world. The Spirit encourages us, builds us up, and heals us through worship and the teaching of the Word. God gets us out of our own heads and amplifies our joy because we're sharing it with others who also are relying on Him. These things can't happen anywhere else.

People have all kinds of reasons for attending church less often these days. Without invalidating some of those concerns, let's remember the benefits of church and not give up on gathering. We have only one life to be on a mission with God. Let's take advantage of this precious season, lock shields with our brothers and sisters, and see what He does.

....

....

....

....

....

....

APPLY

What do you see as the value of church?

How has God used other believers to help, build, and heal you?

PRAY

DATE: ....

PRAISE GOD FOR RESTORATION

READ PSALM 68:1–10

UNDERSTAND

Today's scripture reading asks readers to shift the way they look at others and what they expect from God. While God will punish those who rebel, there also is blessing for those who are suffering. Perhaps it's easy to overlook those who are suffering—or even to view them as afflicted—but God's desire is for the restoration of those who are most vulnerable.

The place where you can begin today is praise for God for His mercy and restoration. Just as God provided for the people of Israel in the wilderness and restored their lives, He desires to help those who are weighed down and burdened today. You don't have to be worthy on your own in order to approach God with confidence and hope. God always looks to those in the greatest need in order to show His mercy.

Look around today at those who are most in need or suffering. These are the people God wants to help and to restore. As you praise God for His mercy and justice, you can also shift your own view of suffering and seek ways to draw near to those who are at the heart of God's desires.

....

....

....

....

....

....

....

APPLY

How does God treat those who are suffering and desolate?

....

....

....

How could praising God change the way His people view others?

....

....

....

PRAY

....

....

....

DATE: ....

WRESTLING WITH GOD

READ GENESIS 32:24–32

UNDERSTAND

Jacob was a religious dude from a religious family. All his life, he had heard about his dad's and his grandfather's encounters with God—the miraculous deliverances, the life-changing tests of faith, the blessings of provision and purpose. And yet, from the moment of his birth, Jacob's behavior was characterized by sneakiness, lies, and thievery.

God wasn't real to him. While Jacob had no reason to doubt the stories his dad and grandpa told, for him, that's all they were—stories. Jacob did what was required to honor God, at least superficially, and that was enough for him. But that wasn't enough for God.

God literally got in his face and grappled with him because He knew that's what it would take to break through Jacob's self-reliance—and boy, did He break through! Once Jacob realized whom he was battling, he wouldn't let go until God blessed him, though he didn't walk away unscathed. God touched Jacob's hip, and pop! Jacob walked with a limp for the rest of his life.

Hardship and hard questions remind you that God exists and that He wants you to seek Him. Let Him cut away everything keeping you from really knowing Him, even if what He prunes seems like a good thing. If you trust Him no matter what, you've moved from religion to relationship. Don't let go until He blesses you.

....

....

....

....

....

APPLY

When has God used something hard to draw you closer to Him?

How relentless are you in seeking God's blessing?

PRAY

DATE: ....

USE WHAT GOD HAS GIVEN TO YOU

READ MATTHEW 25:14–30

UNDERSTAND

You may not believe that you have a lot to offer God or other people, but if you view your talents, abilities, and possessions as gifts from the Lord, then you have no reason to neglect them. Even the slightest ability or smallest portion of free time can be used well to serve or bless others. God has chosen to bless others through your abilities. In addition, He will increase what you have so that you can reach more people for His purposes.

The wicked and lazy servant in this parable didn't use the gifts God had given him and didn't have any plans to use them. The main issue here is neglect. If you neglect what God has given you, why should He give you anything else?

If you desire to be useful to God and a blessing to others, just ask Him to open your eyes to what He's given you, including the abilities you can use for Him. There are opportunities around you right now, and God wants you to use what He's given you to bless others and glorify Him.

....

....

....

....

....

....

....

APPLY

What has God given to you?

How can you "invest" the gifts God has given you?

PRAY

DATE: ....

GOD LOVES AN UNDERDOG

READ 2 CORINTHIANS 5:14–19

UNDERSTAND

We know God loves an underdog—just look at David, chosen because, as 1 Samuel 16:7 (MSG) declares, "GOD judges persons differently than humans do. Men and women look at the face; GOD looks into the heart."

David's whole story, though, reveals the trap we often fall into as Christians: We come to faith because we see ourselves properly in relation to God, as massive underdogs. Then we get comfortable being on the winning side and start to view ourselves as favorites, like the job's done. That's where David got into trouble; he got comfortable and took his favored status with God for granted.

To live life well, we need a growing relationship with Jesus. We must make a priority of what matters most to Him—seeking the highest good of as many others as we can to help populate His kingdom. As Paul noted in 2 Corinthians 5:14 (ESV), "The love of Christ controls us."

Jesus died for everyone so that as many as possible can live for Him. Since God doesn't see us the way the world does, we can't look at anyone else the way the world does. So no quick judgments, no assuming the worst—only the effort to see others through God's eyes of love and grace.

....

....

....

....

....

....

APPLY

Do you prefer underdogs or favorites?

What do you think it means to let the love of Christ control you?

PRAY

DATE: ....

HIGHER WAYS, HIGHER THOUGHTS

READ ISAIAH 55:6–11

UNDERSTAND

Only a dishonest Christian says he has never been disappointed with God's response to a prayer. There is an ebb and flow to walking with God, times when He feels wonderfully near and others when He seems nowhere to be found. When you're in the groove with God, nothing's better. Why can't it be like that all the time?

The Bible makes it clear that God is always near. We're the ones who move away from Him. Maybe He allows it for a season and a purpose, the way He did in Genesis 40 when Joseph was seemingly forgotten in jail. Or maybe we've slipped and He's course-correcting us.

When we believe that we have God figured out and then He does something we don't understand, it's easy to become bitter. Some even leave the faith because they think God's view of people is less loving, less righteous, and less merciful than theirs. But we cannot forget who God is, that even in our confusion and frustration, He never wastes our pain and He never forsakes us.

No matter how far you have drifted from Him, turn to Him without hesitation or reservation. Isaiah 55:7 (NLT) says God "will forgive generously." He just wants you back on board.

....

....

....

....

....

....

APPLY

Have you ever felt let down by God? How did you get back on track with Him?

What is the difference between certainty in what God does and trust in who God is?

PRAY

DATE: ....

EFFECTIVE WISDOM

READ ECCLESIASTES 9:13–18

UNDERSTAND

Wisdom is a powerful resource that comes from God's Spirit and can bring many benefits. While you likely aren't tasked with saving a city from an attacking army, the wisdom of God can have a tremendous impact in your life—if you value it and seek it out as if it were a precious treasure that could change everything for you.

Wisdom is a quiet power; it's easily neglected and even scorned by followers of those who lead with loud shouts and agitating comments. Wisdom is often valued most when you need it desperately. But when other concerns take over in life, wisdom can fall by the wayside.

One of the most compelling reasons to cling to the wisdom of God is the potential damage sin can do. One sinner can destroy a lot of good, and so can one sin. Wisdom can help you spot the threats to your stability in the Lord. Without God's steady hand of wisdom guiding you forward, it's all the more likely that you'll go astray from His path for your life. But when you heed and live in His wisdom, He'll keep you on course.

APPLY

Why is wisdom considered better than strength but many still neglect it?

How do the shouts of a "ruler of fools" (verse 17 NIV) drown out the quiet words of the wise?

PRAY

DATE: ....

ON THE STRAIGHT AND NARROW

READ LUKE 13:24–27

UNDERSTAND

What difference does it make if we (or others) believe in God or not? Do the details of our spirituality really matter? Wouldn't it be easier to just let folks live the best lives they can?

At first, yes, much easier. However, that way of thinking and living is what Jesus called the wide gate "that leads to destruction" (Matthew 7:13 NIV). If all those people were being honest, they would probably agree that, for all their virtuous behavior, life's meaning is still confusing and going with the flow is ultimately empty. But they still dismiss God as a solution. Ultimately, God will honor their free will by giving them an eternity without Him.

But what do we do with Luke 13:27 (NKJV), where we see people who call themselves Christians being rejected by Jesus as "workers of iniquity"? Luke 13 points to the heart of the problem—the appearance of righteousness versus actual righteousness.

God alone knows the difference because He alone is truly righteous. That's why the gate that leads to life is narrow—the width of a Man hanging on a cross. Only Jesus walked a straight and true path—the one He paved for any who would follow Him. We can't love God without loving His rescue plan or without loving others and wanting to see them get through that skinny gate.

....

....

....

....

....

....

APPLY

What parts of worldly thinking and living do you find most attractive?

....

....

....

....

....

....

....

....

....

....

....

....

In what area of your life is it hardest to submit to God?

....

....

....

....

....

....

....

....

....

....

....

....

PRAY

....

....

....

....

....

....

DATE: ....

THE ROOT OF FEAR

READ PSALM 34:1–9; 1 SAMUEL 21:10, 22:2

UNDERSTAND

David wrote Psalm 34 when Saul tried to kill him. Saul was jealous that God had chosen someone else to be king. Both men were reacting to frightening situations, but the contrast between their responses is telling.

David faced trouble by relying on God, but Saul chose his own devices, which separated him more and more from God. David feared God more than men; it was the opposite for Saul. David cared more about what God thought of him than his reputation or standing before people, even though it meant going on the run; Saul chose expedience at every turn. In the end, only David had the strength to stand.

For so many men, fear is one of their strongest motivators. We're afraid of failure, often of intimacy, and of being revealed to be a fraud (especially when we've been successful). We avoid situations where we might not succeed because we're afraid our failures would define us. We don't let people get to know us because they might reject us. We don't dare admit we don't know how to do something at work because our boss might think it was a bad move to promote us. But God has more for us than that.

David admitted he was afraid and gave the situation to God, who helped him get through it and ultimately vindicated him. When you hold nothing back from God, fear loses its grip and faith takes hold.

....

....

....

....

APPLY

What frightens you the most?

When was the last time you worried about people's opinions more than God's?

PRAY

DATE: ....

JUST KEEP PLOWING

READ HOSEA 10:12–13

UNDERSTAND

Hosea is one of those no-holds-barred Old Testament prophets who made it clear that if even God's people reject Him long enough, He will let them have what they want. Case in point, the Babylonian exile—one of the lowest points in Israel's history. Hosea 10:13 (NKJV) describes the root of all Israel's sins: "You have eaten the fruit of lies, because you trusted in your own way."

Only God can insert a ray of hope into a message of dire judgment and mean it. But the fact that He does should inspire us to keep hope's flame burning in a darkening world. Even as Israel's doom was laid out, Hosea passed along a message of hope: Hosea 10:12's promise of God's faithfulness at all times. When we seek God's righteousness, He is faithful to bless us with all we need to do His work.

That's the only hopeful verse in a chapter of violent darkness, but it reminds us that no matter how overwhelmingly bad things get, God's light is never completely extinguished. Your part is to keep plowing the fields, to keep sowing His good news, especially when the light seems dimmest. Remind yourself and others that as bad as things may get, God has provided a harvest—hope now and life forever.

....

....

....

....

....

....

APPLY

How regularly do you rely on God's righteousness to give you faith in hard times?

How often do you think of your role as God's ambassador in the world?

PRAY

DATE: ....

HOW TO USE YOUR FREEDOM

READ 1 CORINTHIANS 10:23–24

UNDERSTAND

John 8:36 (NLT) shows us that an effective witness begins with the liberation Christ purchased for us: "If the Son sets you free, you are truly free." Being set free from sin is all-encompassing: We are new creations in Christ, raised with Him from the dead spiritual state we were born into. Not only do we have His power in us to stop our bad habits, but we are also free from fitting into the world's mold.

That freedom, however, carries responsibility. God's grace reminds us to treat others the way He treats us, with respect for our free will and a relentless desire for our highest good. His Spirit in us inspires and strengthens us to obey out of love, from the same position of humility Jesus assumed with us. After all, Jesus needed nothing when He came from heaven to rescue us. He did so because He wanted to please the Father and build a bridge to reunite God with His creation.

Stay mindful of how your choices in nonessential matters impact other believers. Err on the side of caution out of love, and as Paul said in 1 Corinthians 10:31 (NLT), "Whatever you do, do it all for the glory of God."

....

....

....

....

....

....

....

APPLY

What has Christ set you free from, both generally and personally?

When is it hardest to put others' needs ahead of your own? What makes it difficult?

PRAY

DATE: ....

GOD RESPONDS TO CHANGES OF HEART

READ JONAH 3–4

UNDERSTAND

Jonah didn't hold out much hope for the people of Nineveh, and their change of heart after hearing the prophet preach was shocking. No matter how far you may have drifted from God, no matter how grievously you've sinned against God, and no matter how much shame you carry, you couldn't top the people of Nineveh. They were so wicked that God threatened to destroy their city.

But the Ninevites had a change of heart and repented. . .and God spared them.

God doesn't overlook a change of heart. If you come to God in repentance today, He will most certainly have mercy on you. There is no point too far from God. The psalms speak of mourning being turned into dancing, and such a turnaround is always possible when God's people confess their sins and seek Him again.

When God saw the Ninevites' change of heart, He had mercy on them. But Jonah, who had reason to dislike the people of Nineveh, was angry because he hoped God would destroy them for their wickedness. Don't be like Jonah! Instead, when you learn that someone—even the worst sinner, the type of sinner who has ruined the lives of others—has a change of heart toward God, join all the angels in heaven in rejoicing over that saved soul!

....

....

....

....

....

APPLY

In what ways did the people of Nineveh have more faith in God than Jonah did?

What kinds of changes did the king of Nineveh demand for his people?

PRAY

DATE: ....

WAITING ON JUSTICE, LIVING OUT MERCY

READ PSALM 9:1–10

UNDERSTAND

Compassion fatigue is real, and it can limit our desire for justice. The world is such a mess that it's easier not to care. The alternative—getting too deep in the weeds of daily headlines and the trials and problems of others—is no better. But there is more for the Christian than a seesaw between apathy and anger, and it starts with God.

Psalm 9 reminds us that God is paying attention to current events, as He has throughout history. He isn't blowing stuff off, and His temper isn't like ours—a cartoon thermometer boiling into the red with explosive fury. His anger at sin is righteous and just—and yet, He is always good and loving. He also has knowledge and perspective we don't, and our only real decision is whether we're going to trust Him to do what's right.

God "will judge the world with justice," but He is also "a shelter for the oppressed, a refuge in times of trouble" (Psalm 9:8–9 NLT). He perfectly strikes the proper balance of truth and love at all times and in all situations. Neither the times you've been wronged nor the times you've wronged others have escaped His notice. And whenever He chooses to deal with those injustices is the right time, whether in this life or the next.

....

....

....

....

....

APPLY

How do you tend to see God's attitude toward people—as one of wrath or of grace?

How does your view of God impact your heart toward people?

PRAY

DATE: ....

GETTING TO THE HEART OF WHAT MATTERS

READ GALATIANS 1:10–12

UNDERSTAND

Tests are God's way of making sure you understand that following Christ was never meant to be comfortable or undertaken without consideration for what it will cost you. Just as it cost God everything to save you, you must decide what you will give up to follow Him.

At the heart of every test is the issue of surrender. What is God asking you to surrender to Him? Questions of evil and injustice? Bitterness over the hypocrisy you see in your church? Is it the feeling of God's absence at a critical moment?

When Paul said, "If I were still trying to be popular with men, I would not be a servant of Christ," it's clear that the heart of his conversion hinged on sorting out what mattered most to him. He was basically the same man, but his view of God had changed. He reordered his priorities, putting God first instead of his own accomplishments, views, background, or questions.

Because Paul saw God differently, he saw himself differently, and he learned to see others with fresh eyes. When what matters most to God matters most to you, your heart will change, and so will your corner of the world.

....

....

....

....

....

....

APPLY

What does putting God first look like?

When have you put your desire to please people over your desire to please God?

PRAY

DATE: ....

TAMING THE GREEN-EYED MONSTER

READ DEUTERONOMY 4:23–24

UNDERSTAND

We get nervous when we read that God is jealous. It's one of mankind's worst traits, so how could it possibly be any part of God's character? But dozens of verses speak of Him this way.

Here's the difference: God is jealous for His good name and for His people's hearts. He is jealous because He is holy, loving what He loves and hating what He hates with a purity of purpose and passion we cannot imagine.

Human jealousy is driven by envy—the selfish lust for what someone else has because we want to be superior in things like material goods, relationships, or reputation.

How, then, do we fight our jealousy? As 1 Corinthians 6:19–20 (NIV) says, if you call Jesus Lord and Savior, "you are not your own; you were bought at a price." Jesus thus reserves the right to burn away everything that keeps you from being fully unified with Him. Christ's sacrifice consumes all your old ways, including your envy.

God wants us to want Him more than anything or anyone else. When we do, His Spirit in us purifies our desires and intentions. Over time, we learn to distinguish between our harmful, futile envy and His relentless, jealous love. With His help, we practice putting others' needs ahead of our own, wanting God's best for them more than anything else.

....

....

....

....

APPLY

What makes you jealous?

What do you think of when God says He is jealous?

PRAY

DATE: ....

GOD HAS YOUR BACK

READ HEBREWS 2:14–18

UNDERSTAND

To be human is to be tempted. Even Jesus was tempted by Satan, which tells us that temptation itself isn't a sin. Our response is what matters, and often we forget who God is and what He has done to help us overcome our struggles with our flesh, the world, and the devil.

God limits the strength of temptation so you can bear it, and He gives you a way out (1 Corinthians 10:13). Even so, expect a struggle. Jesus died to set you free, but He suffered to do it. Jesus didn't want the cup of God's wrath, but He knew that God would provide the way through and that the reward (which includes you) would be worth the pain.

Jesus knows what it's like to stare down temptation. Hebrews 4:15–16 (NLT) assures us, "He faced all of the same testings we do, yet he did not sin. So let us come boldly to the throne of our gracious God. There we will receive his mercy, and we will find grace to help us when we need it most." "Come boldly" means to cry out to God with expectation—and to believe that no matter how strong the impulse is, He will help you fight and overcome it. Pray, fast, read scripture, and keep seeking His face till the terrible moment passes. Like Jesus, you will have to suffer to conquer temptation—but you can.

....

....

....

....

....

....

APPLY

What temptations most often befall you? What keeps you from asking God for help?

What is your expectation when you ask God to help you overcome temptation?

PRAY

DATE: ....

GOD'S JUSTICE WILL WIN

READ HABAKKUK 2:12–20

UNDERSTAND

The prophet Habakkuk warned his audience that the consequences for their reliance on false gods would soon be visited upon them. That message also applies today.

There is no escaping the moment when God returns to earth in order to set things right. What you invest in today will be revealed for what it is on the day Jesus returns. There is no deceiving God, and so your best option is to seek Him with all your heart.

Consider that while some call out to their idols for help, the followers of the Lord are told to be silent before the temple. The Lord is present in the earth even if you can't see Him or look at an image of Him. You can only trust in faith that the Lord is with you and that you can't do anything to make Him more real or more present. The Lord will act to save His people and to bring justice to the earth, and nothing can stand in His way when the time comes.

As you pray today, consider where you place your trust and what you rely on. Then, seek God's presence with quiet confidence. You don't have to shout in order for God to hear you. In fact, you may not need to say anything at all.

....

....

....

....

....

....

....

APPLY

Why would people create idols and then rely on them for their security and prosperity?

What are some examples of modern idols that people may rely on to save them?

PRAY

DATE: ....

TAKE TIME TO REMEMBER

READ PSALM 105:1–11

UNDERSTAND

Psalm 105 praises God by looking back at the first part of His history with Israel. We see the pattern God established at creation and continues through this very day in the church age: taking barren hearts and making something fruitful. God looked at formless chaos and spoke the world and everything in it into existence.

Then He built a nation out of an unlikely bunch of wanderers and called it His own, putting Israel at the center of redemptive history. Jesus chose to be born into poverty and assembled a motley crew to spread His good news, changing the world. That's where you come in. You are a part of God's story, through His grace and love a saint and coheir with Christ, and He has important things for you to do.

Throughout God's dealings with us is the command to remember. When God-centered things happened to saints of old, they built monuments. They celebrated God's triumph, whether by building piles of stones, celebrating high holy days, or recalling God's deeds in worship.

What are the monuments marking your history with God? Part of pursuing God is recalling His faithfulness. Find ways to remind yourself to thank and praise Him. Whatever you do, remember Him on those dates.

....

....

....

....

....

....

APPLY

You're a part of God's history with all mankind. How does that make you feel?

How do you celebrate when God does something significant in your life?

PRAY

DATE: ....

GRACE UPON GRACE

READ JOHN 1:14–16

UNDERSTAND

The wonder of Jesus' exchange on the cross is that He got all the bad stuff our sinful nature and behavior deserve, while we receive everything He deserves. As Ephesians 2:8–9 says, salvation is an undeserved, unexpected gift given by grace.

But God's favor doesn't stop when you receive Christ; it's only beginning. Once you are under the power of grace instead of sin, you should expect a constant outpouring of what John called Christ's "fullness" (John 1:16 NIV). As James 4:6 (ESV) puts it, throughout our time with Jesus, "he gives more grace." Grace includes God seeing us through the lens of Jesus' righteousness.

If God pouring out grace upon grace on you makes you feel unworthy, remember that's how grace works. God sees what you are becoming—the image of Christ. Let God bless you, cover you, favor you, and be delighted with you—because He wants you to share the overflow of His grace with others.

Imagine a heart so full of His grace that you bless your enemies, that you speak God's redeeming truth to someone who has spoken lies about you. You are His beloved son, and He is pleased with you. Let that truth encourage you to see others through that grace-filled lens.

....

....

....

....

....

....

APPLY

How does God's love affect your behavior on a daily basis?

How hard is it for you to accept things you haven't earned?

PRAY

DATE: ....

NO MORE CAT-AND-MOUSE

READ LUKE 11:1–13

UNDERSTAND

Prayer is challenging because it reminds us of our reliance on God. When things are going well, it's human nature to leave prayer for meal times, because hey, things are going well. When things are *not* going well, we often complain first, try to place blame somewhere, or work on fixing the issue—leaving prayer as a last resort: "Well, I guess the only thing we can do now is pray."

When we fail to pray as a first option—to avail ourselves of our Christ-bought access to God—we default to self-sufficiency. And then we blame God when we're not enough. That suggests we aren't really trusting God—at least, not more than we trust ourselves. We treat God like a good backup plan.

Often too, we end up trying to game God with our prayers—to make sure we're using the right-sounding words, to pester Him like creditors seeking payment. We fear an answer of "wait" or "no," as if a "yes" means God is finally seeing things the way we think they should be.

But when Jesus taught His followers to pray, He encouraged the boldness and persistence that comes from a healthy relationship. We are sons, and God is our Father. Our prayer life should reflect that basic attitude.

....

....

....

....

....

....

APPLY

How hard is prayer for you? What makes it difficult?

What do you think God's best for you is?

PRAY

DATE: ....

WORSHIP ON MANUAL

READ 1 CHRONICLES 16:1–4, 8–12, 34–36

UNDERSTAND

In 1 Chronicles 16, David brought the ark to Jerusalem for the first time, placed it in the tabernacle as the focal point of God's presence, and led a God-honoring celebration that ended with the people shouting "amen" and praising the Lord. God was front and center, and all hearts were focused on Him.

If only all of our worship times could be like that! Too often, we get stuck on music style or song length, or we just get bored and go through the motions. Regardless of our feelings, we should always bear in mind that God is looking for "those who worship Him. . .in spirit and truth" (John 4:24 NKJV).

Even David didn't just automatically get it right—in fact, not too long before this glorious moment, he had messed up royally when Israel didn't follow God's specific instructions about bringing the ark back to Jerusalem, and as a result, someone died (2 Samuel 6:6–7).

First Chronicles 16 shows us that David did it right the second time. The hard lesson he learned is that God reserves the right to tell us how He wants to be worshipped. The next time you're feeling itchy about worship, engage your heart first. Are you seeking to worship God His way? He deserves all your attention.

....

....

....

....

....

....

APPLY

Aside from church services, when do you usually make time to worship God?

Do you ever find yourself worshipping on autopilot?

PRAY

DATE: ....

ENDURANCE COMES FROM GOD'S POWER

READ COLOSSIANS 1:1–14

UNDERSTAND

Endurance and patience for the trials of life aren't the kinds of things that come naturally. These are fruits of the Spirit that God can develop in you provided you actively seek them out and ask for them. The strength that God passes on to you has a divine source; you can't earn or develop it through willpower. Endurance, patience, strength—these are all gifts that are given to you based on God's grace.

Although these gifts come through grace, meaning God's unmerited favor, don't overlook the fact that Paul still prayed for these things to be manifested among the Colossian Christians. Being among God's people isn't a guarantee that you'll have instant access to all that God has made available to you. This is where intercession and requests are so important.

Jesus assured you that if you seek, you will find, and He promised that all who are thirsty will be satisfied (Matthew 7:7–8; John 4:14). Paul's prayer is an invitation for you to actively seek more from God and to fully explore all you have been given through Jesus.

....

....

....

....

....

....

....

APPLY

How can you grow in your strength and endurance?

How does giving thanks to God the Father in difficulties help you persevere?

PRAY

DATE: ....

THE MIRROR DOESN'T LIE

READ JAMES 4:1–10

UNDERSTAND

James' writing is great because he is so blunt and practical. You don't go to James for a spiritual hug, but for an unblinking look at how you're living out your faith. You read James expecting a little course correction—and he doesn't disappoint.

Look at his verbs in James 4:7–10 (NKJV): *submit, resist, draw near, cleanse, purify, lament* and *mourn* and *weep, humble yourselves.* These are strong verbs, demanding wholehearted action. It's no surprise, coming from the guy who told us to view trouble as an opportunity for joy (James 1:2) and who warned us that our own ungodly desires eventually conceive and deliver death (James 1:13–15).

James is like an Old Testament prophet, a tough voice bringing hard words that remind us that God's grace saves us from hell. Works don't save us, but they do show our faith—our belief that in following Christ, we have found the best, most meaningful, and ultimately most satisfying way to live.

If Jesus isn't making a difference in the choices you make, in the actions you take, then James says you need to take a hard look at your faith. Is your trust in God or in yourself?

....

....

....

....

....

....

....

APPLY

How has God shown His love and loyalty to you?

What makes it hard for you to offer those virtues to Him in return?

PRAY

DATE: ....

SEEKING A HEART OF FORGIVENESS

READ HOSEA 3:1–5

UNDERSTAND

Hosea had one of the toughest assignments of all the Old Testament prophets: to marry a woman and have children, knowing she was going to cheat on him, time and time again—the same way Israel kept stepping out on God by worshipping false deities.

Even though Hosea knew the pain was coming, he had a job to do. His ministry to Israel meant telling them about God's anger and coming punishment for their lack of faith.

When someone has wronged you, regardless of whether you continue in relationship with that person, the first and hardest move is to forgive. You can't do it alone. Invite trusted, godly men into your pain; ask them to listen and then to help pray you through it until you're ready to take that step of obedience and forgive that person.

If you're the causer of the pain, the pattern is similar: Seek to make things right, putting the power to forgive in the other person's hands. Sometimes, that person won't want to make things right. Do all you can, and then trust God with the outcome.

....

....

....

....

....

....

....

APPLY

What is the deepest relationship wound you've ever suffered?

What's the worst sin you've ever committed? Did you seek forgiveness?

PRAY

DATE: ....

PAIN'S HARVEST

READ HEBREWS 12:5–13

UNDERSTAND

The human capacity for endurance and pain tolerance is impressive, but it helps to have someone who's been there telling you what to expect, honing your skills and encouraging you to press on. For the Christian, that's Jesus.

Jesus endured hostility and apathy, rejection and betrayal—culminating at the cross—because as Hebrews 12:2 (NKJV) says, He kept His eyes on "the joy that was set before Him": the goal of bringing as many people as would accept Him into the unity and harmony of relationship with God. He leaned into the brokenness of this world with the long-term goal of redeeming and restoring it, and He expects us to do the same. The pursuit of God revolves around letting Him teach us more about and guide us deeper into His truth, even (and especially) during painful times.

Hebrews 12:11 (NLT) offers a promise that God's chastening has a reward: "a peaceful harvest of right living for those who are trained in this way." Because of Jesus, we are part of the new covenant in His blood, bonded by His forgiveness and His promise to never leave nor forsake us. Because of this, we can endure pain, knowing it will pass and that His eternal purposes are in it.

....

....

....

....

....

....

APPLY

What qualities do you respect most in a mentor, coach, or teacher?

What is your initial reaction to being redirected or challenged to improve?

PRAY

DATE: ....

YOUR RESPONSE TO SCRIPTURE

READ DANIEL 9:1–19

UNDERSTAND

Do you remember who always rides along with you? Imagine asking the Lord, "Would You please read today's passage to me?" Jesus smiles and says yes. When He finishes, He doesn't close your Bible and give it back to you. Instead, He looks at you and smiles again.

You wait expectantly, but the Lord doesn't say anything. Then it occurs to you, *Oh, He wants me to say something. He wants to know my response to what He just spoke to my heart.*

The easiest response is to pray: "Lord, I thank You for Daniel 9:2–3, which says, 'I, Daniel, learned from reading the word of the LORD. . .'"

Even better? To pray: "Lord, I thank You for Daniel 9:2–3, which tells me that Daniel read a portion of the book of Jeremiah, took that portion's sober and hope-filled truths to heart, and then turned to You in earnest, serious, and wholehearted prayer."

In the end, all Bible study is a conversation. It's the Lord speaking to your heart and then you responding in prayer. That's why every Bible study in this book ends with a time of prayer!

....

....

....

....

....

....

....

....

APPLY

How easy or difficult is it for you to take God at His word?

What would make it easier for you?

PRAY

DATE: ....

SET YOUR HEART

READ 1 CHRONICLES 22

UNDERSTAND

What David did in arranging for the temple to be built foreshadowed what God is doing now in the church age. Instead of a single building and center of worship, however, God's presence and power are found in every individual who believes in the name of God's Son. Instead of drawing believers to a single place in Jerusalem, He is reaching the world through the gospel so voices from all nations can be raised in worship.

The heart of worship, however, remains the same: "Set your heart and your soul to seek the LORD your God" (1 Chronicles 22:19 NKJV). *Set* in Hebrew means to give with a determined purpose in mind. In context, it points to David's instructions to honor God wholeheartedly—to put Him first—and to seek His help in building a place to honor Him above all else.

If you belong to Him body and soul, you're engaging in kingdom building. You're acting as His temple, bringing people to seek and worship God for themselves, some with refreshed hearts and others for the first time.

....

....

....

....

....

....

....

....

APPLY

What does it look like to give yourself completely to God?

How do Bible study and worship help you put God first?

PRAY

DATE: ....

DO YOU WANT TO BE HEALED?

READ JOHN 5:2–9

UNDERSTAND

Jesus cut right to the heart of the matter with the sick man at the pool of Bethesda: "Do you want to be healed?" (John 5:6 ESV). Excuses were all he offered in reply—someone always beat him to the pool, no one helped him, and so on. What did Jesus know about this man that we don't?

Sometimes we get so used to a bad situation—a chronic illness or depression or anxiety—that we think God has lost interest in us. Or we think maybe God's grace isn't actually enough. God can handle honest doubt, but it's a mistake to hang on to doubt because we think it's all we have.

When God brings something like that to your attention, deal with it. If you can accept His redirection, no matter what it is, He will give you the grace and strength to move on. Let the Spirit guide you, bearing in mind Paul's words in Romans 8:26 (NKJV): "We do not know what we should pray for as we ought, but the Spirit Himself makes intercession for us."

....

....

....

....

....

....

....

....

APPLY

How did God answer the last big request you made of Him?

What does it mean to pray with expectation?

PRAY

DATE: ....

ARE YOUR PRIORITIES CORRECT?

READ 1 CORINTHIANS 13

UNDERSTAND

Paul knew that the Corinthians loved higher learning and spectacular spiritual gifts such as prophecy. While he certainly valued these things, he rightly worried that they had put their emphasis in the wrong place.

Consider today what you truly value. What is really important to you in your everyday life, especially your spiritual life? It's easy to get sidetracked by lesser priorities and to make side issues really serious sticking points that sow division in the church, which can cause different groups to take sides, choose leaders, and attack one another endlessly.

Paul's higher road involves faith, hope, and love, things he said would last forever. Faith means living each day in total dependence on God. Hope is a sense of unseen clarity about the future that places it in God's hands. Love, the greatest of the three, means both acceptance by a merciful God and an accepting, compassionate heart attitude toward fellow believers. We should never be so focused on gaining knowledge or spiritual gifts that we miss out on faith, hope, and love.

....

....

....

....

....

....

....

....

APPLY

What is the correct balance between the pursuit of spiritual gifts and the pursuit of love?

....

....

....

....

....

....

....

....

....

....

....

....

How did Paul find comfort despite all the things he didn't know or understand?

....

....

....

....

....

....

....

....

....

....

....

....

PRAY

....

....

....

....

....

....

DATE: ....

NO FAKING IT

READ ZEPHANIAH 2:1–3

UNDERSTAND

Zephaniah's prophecies rained down hard, proclaiming "the day of the Lord" more than any other Old Testament prophet—God's wrath coming down through the ages on all who reject His ways. One particularly frightening warning comes in Zephaniah 2:3 (NIV): If God's people will humble themselves, do what God commands, and pursue righteousness, "perhaps [they] will be sheltered on the day of the LORD's anger." Perhaps they'll be sheltered? What's that about?

In Matthew 7:21–23, Jesus referred to people who call themselves Christians, and even behave like Christians, but will not be saved. They won't realize this until it's too late, when they are rejected by Jesus when He returns to judge the earth. As He said, "All you did was use me to make yourselves important. You don't impress me one bit. You're out of here" (verse 23 MSG).

Some men go to church for a long time before they actually become Christians. Unless a man gives himself fully to God, letting his maker do as He wants in his heart, he builds his life on sand. You know you're His when you'll do anything to become more like Jesus—including giving up habits, coming clean, and enduring temporary shame because you want to get right with Him.

....

....

....

....

....

....

APPLY

How do you show God that He has your whole heart?

Does the thought of God's wrath scare you? Why or why not?

PRAY

DATE: ....

CHOSEN TO BE FRUITFUL

READ JOHN 15:9–17

UNDERSTAND

Jesus set up His statement in John 15:16 by talking about vines and branches (John 15:1–8). The analogy establishes Jesus as the true vine—the source of eternal life—and the Father as the vinedresser, determining which grafted-on branches are fruitful and which aren't. Once we are connected to God through Jesus, our responsibility is to bear fruit—to obey God's commands with humility and compassion.

In John 15:9 (NKJV) Jesus said, "Abide in My love." Clearly, God doesn't force our obedience. In that sense, we must cooperate with Him to fully work out His will for our lives. He knows who is going to receive His offer of salvation, but we still have to choose Him.

Jesus chooses to invest Himself in us, wanting to see us grow in godly love, and He tells us how to do so. In response, we obey His call to spread the good news and to lovingly serve others. That's God's definition of fruitfulness. As we abide in Christ, we are able to pray correctly, asking God in Jesus' name for things that are within His will and will bring Him glory.

....

....

....

....

....

....

....

....

APPLY

How do you think God defines love?

What does loving God look like to you?

PRAY

DATE: ....

GOD'S PURPOSE WILL ALWAYS BE ACCOMPLISHED

READ ACTS 27:14-26

UNDERSTAND

When God has a mission lined up for you, there is nothing on earth that can stand in the way. Paul witnessed that in a most dramatic way while stuck in a life-threatening storm that eventually left him shipwrecked on a remote island. It's easy to get distracted by the circumstances all around you and the reactions of those also in the midst of the storms of life. Others may be giving up all hope, and it can be tempting to follow their lead.

Instead, find confidence in what God has guided you to do and in remaining faithful to it. If your life feels chaotic or directionless, this is the day to quietly seek God's wisdom and guidance. Even if you feel like you're in a storm, God's mission for you cannot be overcome. You'll find peace and security in the assurance of God's calling.

When you enjoy the confidence of God's calling in your life, you can share that peace with others. They can learn to grow in their trust in God as you demonstrate faith and hope in uncertain times.

....

....

....

....

....

....

....

....

APPLY

Why did Paul speak so boldly to the crew of the ship?

Where did Paul tell the crew to find their courage?

PRAY

DATE: ....

THE GREAT PURSUIT

READ ISAIAH 65:1

UNDERSTAND

Story after story recounts God's pursuit of people's hearts, especially when they rejected Him and His ways. The Old Testament is primarily the story of how God picked out one old pagan guy and from him made a nation for Himself, preserving a lineage against all conceivable odds through which He would bring the Messiah and save the world.

Jesus is the face of God's great pursuit. He went out of His way to visit Samaria because He had a divine appointment to bring hope and healing to a woman who had been rejected by her whole community. His parables contain images of a shepherd leaving a whole flock to find one lost sheep, a woman scouring her entire house to find a lost coin, and a man selling all he owned to buy a single pearl worth everything to him.

The theme? You matter to God. He reaches down to you so He can lift you up. You have purpose. God has prepared in advance good works for you to do; and as a Christian, you are now a part of His chosen people. Surely His goodness, mercy, and unfailing love will follow you all the days of your life.

....

....

....

....

....

....

....

APPLY

How did God pursue you to bring you to faith in Christ?

How should you respond, knowing how relentlessly God has sought you?

PRAY

DATE: ....

WHEN GOOD THINGS GO BAD

READ LUKE 16:14–31

UNDERSTAND

In Luke 16, Jesus went right from interpreting the Mosaic law regarding marriage and divorce to the story of a rich man in hell. There's no indication that He shifted to a parable. It reads like a historical account; it feels real.

The story is not about rich people being inherently wicked or the poor being innately good. And even though the possible glimpse into the workings of the afterlife is intriguing, that's not the point either. Jesus was driving at the unique power of His mission regarding one of the greatest worldly challenges to it: the power that comes from having money.

The story of Lazarus and the rich man is a stark illustration of the blinding power of wealth. If we have enough money, we hope we'll be able to avoid life's biggest problems. Money does help; it provides our daily bread and can be an equalizer for many injustices. But when a good thing replaces the best thing in our hearts, it becomes by definition a bad thing.

Unless God is our greatest desire, and our driving ambition is to know and serve Him, nothing will convince us that money and power won't do as well—not even someone rising from the dead.

....

....

....

....

....

....

APPLY

How does the reality of heaven and hell affect the way you live?

How often do you make sure your priorities line up with God's?

PRAY

DATE: ....

LOVE NEVER QUITS

READ 1 JOHN 4:15–21

UNDERSTAND

Love originates with God; as 1 John 4:8 says, He is love. Father, Son, and Holy Spirit have always existed in perfect community and love—love so vital and abundant that God chose to create us to share in His love. There is nothing He could receive from us that would make Him greater, better, or more loving. In other words, He loves because it's who He is.

We are not born knowing how to love. In our natural, sinful condition, all we know is need. We need food, we need shelter, and we need love. More than anything, we want to be loved, and we learn to give love so we can get it. When we run into God's love—love that has everything to offer and nothing to gain from us—we don't know how to respond. It's not in us, but it can be taught, as part of our new nature in Christ.

John gave us insight into loving like God loves. First, we have to accept what it cost for Him to love us—the cross. Once His Spirit is in us, His love begins to move in our hearts, pricking our conscience when we love in the old ways—selfishly, transactionally—and moving us to love others because we love Him.

....

....

....

....

....

....

....

APPLY

What do you think it means to truly love someone?

How has God shown His love for you?

PRAY

DATE: ....

MERCY BELONGS TO EVERYONE

READ MATTHEW 18:21–35

UNDERSTAND

If you come to God in search of mercy and forgiveness, the good news of the gospel is that the Lord is merciful and ready to restore your relationship with Him.

The debt described in the parable in today's scripture reading was impossible to pay back. Although the indebted servant was likely reckless with the money loaned to him, he still had the audacity to ask for forgiveness, and the master had the kindness to grant it. Even a massive debt is within the reach of God's mercy.

Mercy and forgiveness should lead to transformation in how you relate to other imperfect humans. God expects you to dwell on the mercy you have received. So, consider how lost you would be without His mercy, and then extend that same consideration to others who are in your debt.

Forgiving a debt can be costly. You may have to swallow your pride, and you may feel like someone has bested or exploited you in some way. Forgiveness doesn't mean that you need to be taken advantage of again, but you do need to let go of your right to demand some kind of payment for a wrong done to you. Holding on to unforgiveness is certainly a temptation, but it isn't an option when you have received God's mercy on such generous terms.

....

....

....

....

....

....

APPLY

Why does Jesus command that His followers show mercy to others?

How does your treatment of others impact your relationship with God?

PRAY

DATE: ....

LIFE AND DEATH ON THE TIP OF YOUR TONGUE

READ PROVERBS 18:12–24

UNDERSTAND

Words either build or destroy, heal or harm. Wise words satisfy like a good meal, but rash or foolish words crush the spirit. They can be caused by believing lies about yourself and others, or by stuffing feelings until they explode from your mouth and damage hard-to-rebuild trust.

If you don't give authority over your tongue to God, your words will be in a constant state of contradiction. You will speak wisdom as well as foolishness and bring light as well as darkness—often in the same conversation. But one word from God can change everything. His words can tell you where your own speech is driven by the wrong motives—ambition, aggression (and passive aggression), and apathy. As Proverbs 4:23 (NIV) says, "Above all else, guard your heart, for everything you do flows from it."

It's hard to find the right things to say if you're not familiar with the Bible. There is no substitute for God's own words of mercy and grace. The time you spend reading it, praying over it, and studying it is time spent stocking your heart with the vocabulary you need to control your tongue, filter out ungodly voices, and bring God's favor into your relationships.

....

....

....

....

....

APPLY

Do you tend to say what's on your mind, or do you think before you speak?

....

....

....

....

....

....

....

....

....

....

....

....

How often do you ask God to help you find the right thing to say?

....

....

....

....

....

....

....

....

....

....

....

....

PRAY

....

....

....

....

....

....

DATE: ....

WORTH EVERY LOSS TO GAIN

READ MATTHEW 13:44

UNDERSTAND

We often pass by God's kingdom without paying any attention to it. Maybe that's why many of Jesus' parables feature a field—in Matthew 13 alone, we have the sower, the wheat and tares, the mustard seed, and the hidden treasure.

We pass fields as we drive from city to city and from appointment to appointment. Unless we're farmers, we don't pause to think about what might be hidden beneath the ground. More immediate concerns command us, events and problems that reside in plain sight, and that's where our focus and energy go.

Jesus told us in Matthew 6:33 to seek God's kingdom as the top priority in our lives. When we do that, He will provide everything we need to function well in life. Unfortunately, we can easily reverse our priorities, taking the kingdom for granted as we pursue our daily needs.

These parables also remind us of the joy of finding and being found. Jesus was the merchant looking for hidden treasure, keeping His plans a mystery until He sold Himself to accomplish His rescue mission. We are His treasure, and His joy was in giving all He had to win us.

Such love requires a response. Jesus gave up heaven to root in the dirt for us; what are we willing to lose to gain His kingdom?

....

....

....

....

....

APPLY

Is there anything you would lose everything else to keep?

What does it mean to you that God considers you worth dying for?

PRAY

DATE: ....

DO YOU LOVE TO WORRY?

READ MATTHEW 6:25–34

UNDERSTAND

Nobody loves to worry, any more than anyone loves to pay taxes or have a root canal. But maybe the real question is this: Do we love our stuff more than we love God? The way we see God affects the way we do everything else, especially worry.

When we lean into our troubles instead of God, worry replaces worship; in effect, we're saying, "God, I don't think You've got this." We would rather trust our worry than His strength and provision. And that impacts our witness: Who wants to listen to Christians who think their God isn't big enough to handle every problem?

Worry is a warning—a yellow light telling you that a choice is coming up fast. Choice one: Take your worry and turn your concerns over to God, trusting Him to help you get through them. Or choice two: Take your worry as a badge of honor, bravery in the face of God's apparent abandonment—proof that you care more about your problems than God does.

Worry is a sign that you're paying attention, that you care about what's going on. That's good. But if you hang on to that worry, you risk making it an idol. So really, what do you love more, worry or God?

....

....

....

....

....

....

....

APPLY

What worries you the most?

How does worry affect your view of God?

PRAY

DATE: ....

BEARING FRUIT

READ JOHN 15:12–17

UNDERSTAND

Jesus chose you to have a long-lasting impact in this world. That means that you have the tremendous privilege of praying to God as a beloved child as well as the great responsibility to align your desires and will to Jesus' desires and will. God has chosen you to bear fruit for Him. That is a part of your identity as a follower of Jesus.

Jesus is so committed to helping you bear fruit for Him and for the benefit of others that He has given you the privilege of making bold prayer requests in His name. He promises that your heavenly Father will give you what you need to accomplish His purposes—if you simply ask in His name. Such a striking promise brings up a key issue: Are your desires in line with Jesus and His will?

You have incredible access to God the Father because you have been united with Him through Jesus. What are you asking Him to do for you today so that you can bear fruit for Him?

....

....

....

....

....

....

....

....

....

....

APPLY

What did Jesus say is the purpose for your life as His follower?

What condition did Jesus place on prayer requests to the Father?

PRAY

DATE: ....

GETTING YOUR HEART STRAIGHT

READ 1 CHRONICLES 16:7–14

UNDERSTAND

First Chronicles 16 centers on a long psalm (verses 8–36) that David and Asaph wrote as a response to God's greatness and mercies. That's so David, right? The guy was a psalm machine, always ready to burst into song about the Lord. So cool. But David's greatness really lies with his willingness to turn to God and face the music when he messed up. That's when the praise really counts.

When you become aware that you've gotten it wrong in God's eyes, it's easy to try to avoid Him. You're embarrassed because you think you should know better, or you're mad because you think He is being too tough on you. But don't let that keep you from coming to Him. And don't forget to start with praise.

Praising God is the only right move you have under every circumstance. Praise and worship are about Him, not you. He is the one who loves to forgive and reconcile and restore. He takes all your brokenness and makes a straight path back to Him—but you can't see it until you acknowledge Him.

Sing with gratitude for His mercies and faithfulness; sing because He deserves it no matter how you feel. Then watch how your feelings will catch up with your faithful actions.

....

....

....

....

....

....

APPLY

What generally happens when we forget who God is and what He has done?

Do you make a regular habit of praising God?

PRAY

DATE: ....

GODLY SORROW

READ 2 CORINTHIANS 7:2–12

UNDERSTAND

Consider how sorrow over a wrong you've done has impacted you. Perhaps you still feel a lingering sense of regret or shame, so you know that sorrow is hardly a pleasant experience. No one wants to mess up. And being the person who has to point out the failure or misdeeds of another brings a sense of sorrow too.

Paul encouraged us to think of this kind of sorrow as a catalyst for a fresh start. He held that we can move on beyond our failures and the weight of our sorrows if we're willing to go to the Lord and repent. In fact, Paul encouraged us not to dwell on our sorrows, except to look ahead to the ways we can make things right.

Moving beyond your sorrows today is a chance to open your life to God's healing and transformation. If you never want to feel the weight of sorrow again, you can imitate the determination of the Corinthians to change their ways. God is always ready to forgive and to aid those who are willing to turn to Him for a fresh start.

....

....

....

....

....

....

....

....

....

APPLY

What are the benefits that Paul attached to godly sorrow?

How do people typically view sorrow today?

PRAY

DATE: ....

OBEDIENCE OUTSIDE THE BUBBLE

READ PHILIPPIANS 2:12–18

UNDERSTAND

How often are you outside the Christian bubble? In other words, how much of your week do you spend out in the world—away from church and like-minded folks—surrounded by people of different beliefs and backgrounds? What's your attitude toward them? How often do you catch yourself feeling superior to them? Do you let your standards slip because no other believers are around?

The key is obedience. Paul told the Christians in Philippi that it was even more important for them to obey God now that he, the founder of their church, wasn't among them. Philippians 2:12 (NLT) says we must "work hard to show the results of [our] salvation, obeying God with deep reverence and fear."

There's nothing passive about that work. We don't want to give people reason to think less of Him. People can be obnoxious about their objections to Jesus, the church, and Christians in general, but it does no good to respond in kind. When you humble yourself like Paul did, you find the rhythm needed to represent Jesus well.

....

....

....

....

....

....

....

APPLY

What makes it difficult for you to share the good news?

How mindful are you of God getting the glory for your words and actions?

PRAY

DATE: ....

GOD STORIES

READ 2 CORINTHIANS 5:14–21

UNDERSTAND

Because Jesus took on the ultimate pain of being cut off from God, you will never be cut off from Him.

And because Jesus did what He did in the way He did it, we should expect that anything is possible in this life, both good and bad. The good things point to God's promise of life, but even the bad reminds us that God's light will eventually extinguish all darkness. That's the power of grace.

Human history is full of stories of God's grace. What makes these accounts so powerful and poignant is the light shining through in the darkest possible moments—of God pursuing people in POW camps, penitentiaries, and sickbeds and delivering them from despair to hope. God has turned ashes into beauty through failed suicide attempts, averted abortions, horrible sicknesses, and the healing of unimaginable wrongs and insurmountable losses.

Dramatic or not, your God stories are one of your best tools when it comes to sharing the good news. God doesn't waste a drop of pain or sorrow, and He will use yours. Your suffering in His hands supercharges your faith.

....

....

....

....

....

....

....

APPLY

What does God's grace mean to you in light of the worst thing you've ever done?

What story would you tell someone of how God's grace personally impacted your life?

PRAY

DATE: ....

LOOK FOR GOD'S NEW THING

READ ISAIAH 43:14–25

UNDERSTAND

The Lord wants you to remember the things He has done in the past, but we should also be on the lookout for Him to do new things today. God isn't content with you learning about the past and stopping there. Each generation has its own calling to be aware of Him and fresh challenges to meet in the moment.

God's promise to do new things means that you are to remain attentive and aware of what He is doing. Thankfully, it's not up to you to create the new things of God. You only need to remain aware of Him, pay attention, and follow where He leads you. Most importantly, don't be surprised if God's new thing feels uncomfortable or unfamiliar. If anything, that may be a sign that you're on the right track and needing to live by faith even more.

You can find hope in the story of God's people who also had to leave the familiar behind and take up the path He had set before them. The Lord is great and powerful, and He will remain with you through the uncertainty of the days ahead.

....

....

....

....

....

....

....

....

APPLY

How could you begin to expect God to do something new?

How can today's passage help expand your understanding of God's power?

PRAY

DATE: ....

LESSER GODS

READ ROMANS 1:16–31

UNDERSTAND

The second half of Romans 1 is an unflinching description of why the world is so messed up. Ultimately, idols exist because mankind has tried to embody a greater sense of things in single facets, individual representations of the divine that we can wrap our minds around. We try to put God in a box and bring Him down to our finite level, resulting in corrupt, confused minds. In trying to limit Him, we shackle ourselves.

Things that are by themselves good—work, ministry, government and politics, even family—become idols when we make them supreme. When good things become the most important things, we settle for lesser gods, and they fail us constantly. What results is everything wrong with the world—all the hot-button issues and every ugly sin in between.

It's easy to get angry at how badly we've broken what God made good. But being a new creation in Christ means we have to channel that anger into kingdom purposes. People are looking for ultimate meaning in their lives. You have it. Your role is to bring loving truth and truthful love into their day.

APPLY

Based on Romans 1:16–31, what qualifies something as an idol?

How often do you pray for individuals or groups who really make you mad?

PRAY

DATE: ....

A COUNTERCULTURAL LIFE

READ ROMANS 12:9–21

UNDERSTAND

In today's scripture reading, Paul mapped out a series of practices for Christians that are extremely countercultural—and even counterintuitive. Let's look at two of them. Giving generously to those in need and showing hospitality have always been vital to supporting others, but both acts require faith that God will provide for your needs when you remain faithful and take care of others. It's surely more acceptable today to think of ways you can stockpile savings and other assets to protect yourself from uncertainty, but Paul said that Christians should be so devoted to the well-being of others that they give generously of their finances and homes to ensure that fellow Christians receive God's care.

The guiding principle for most of today's passage is to seek the best for others, whether that's sharing in their joys or in their sorrows. Seek the best for others even when they curse you, blessing them in return. As you devote yourself to caring for others, you'll find freedom from the self-centeredness that ensnares so many today, and you'll draw near to God's heart for the world.

....

....

....

....

....

....

....

....

APPLY

How can you show prefer-ence to fellow Christians in brotherly love?

Why is it so important to bless those who perse-cute you and to overcome evil with good?

PRAY

DATE: ....

BLESSINGS IN HARDSHIPS

READ PHILIPPIANS 1:12–20

UNDERSTAND

In Paul's letter to the Philippian church, he described a path to joy, freedom, and blessing that may seem counterintuitive. Yet Paul himself is an example of its effectiveness.

Paul endured suffering very few can even imagine. Yet he never complained but continued doing what God had called him to do—even in the face of sometimes frightening opposition. Through everything, Paul made the gospel and the reputation of Jesus his top priority. Paul is our example of remaining focused on Jesus and His message no matter what it costs.

This isn't to say that you should desire the kinds of struggles Paul endured. You can ask God to protect you from difficulties, but you should also be aware that He can meet you and bless you in the midst of hardship and struggles. God can work in you and for your benefit as well as the benefit of those around you in any life situation.

If you link your desires with God's, you'll have a better perspective on life. The stakes of life will look very different when you care deeply about seeing other people enjoy liberty in Christ. And you'll find it easier to endure suffering and to look for a silver lining in your struggles when you remember that God is with you through whatever you endure.

....

....

....

....

....

....

APPLY

Why would Paul rejoice over his imprisonment?

What was Paul's main goal in his ministry and how did that lead to freedom and joy?

PRAY

CHECK OUT THESE FAITH MAPS FOR THE ENTIRE FAMILY. . .

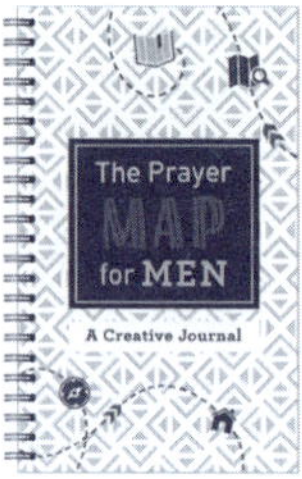

The Prayer Map for Men
978-1-64352-438-2

The Prayer Map for Women
978-1-63609-762-6

The Prayer Map for Women
978-1-63609-763-3

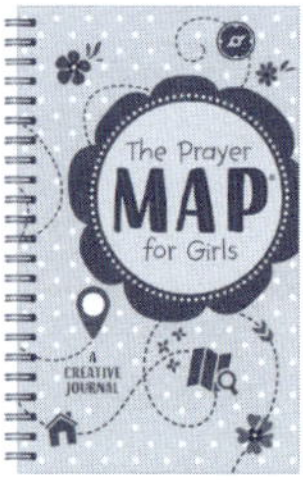

The Prayer Map for Girls
978-1-68322-559-1

The Prayer Map for Boys
978-1-68322-558-4

The Prayer Map for Teens
978-1-68322-556-0

These purposeful prayer journals are a fun and creative way to more fully experience the power of prayer. Each page guides you to write out thoughts, ideas, and lists. . .which then creates a specific "map" for you to follow as you talk to God. Each map includes a spot to record the date, so you can look back on your prayers and see how God has worked in your life. *The Prayer Map* will not only encourage you to spend time talking with God about the things that matter most. . .it will also help you build a healthy spiritual habit of continual prayer for life!

Spiral Bound

Find This and More from Barbour Publishing at Your Favorite Bookstore or www.barbourbooks.com

BARBOUR PUBLISHING

Editor's Note

The farm-to-table idea harkens back to a simpler time when family farms were very common and neighbors helped neighbors within the natural cycle of seasons. When our ancestors migrated to cities over the years and urban living became the norm, farmland was lost to development and the farming way of life was downplayed in importance. Corporate farms took over the task of large-scale production of food, packing and shipping it all over the world.

Today's farm-to-table movement is based on the view that food is freshest and at its best for us when sourced as close to home as possible. By producing your own food or buying it direct from local farms, farmer's markets, CSAs, and the like, you are helping to build food security and strengthening community bonds. It reduces the time between harvest and when you can eat the food, increasing taste and quality while reducing the energy costs of transportation across the country—or world.

In this cookbook, we'll include recipes that feature dairy, fruits, meats, and vegetables that are commonly available from farms in the Mid-Atlantic and Midwest of the United States near the largest Amish communities.

To find local farm-to-table food sources, you can search the internet for farms near you where you can purchase direct, buy a herd share, or pick your own produce. Using social media to connect with farms and farmer's markets will often give you inside information on how the food is grown. Invite neighbors to swap garden produce with you and ask friends where to find the best farmstands.

Whenever you prepare a farm-to-table meal, you can be assured you are doing your part for your family's health, your community's strength, and, ultimately, the planet's well-being.

GROWING UP *on a* FARM

I have many good memories of living on a farm as a child. I had eleven siblings and bonus grandparents who lived in a *dawdy* house adjoining our big house.

Going to town with grandpa was so fun, and he always made sure we each got a turn to go. He always bought us a treat, like an ice cream bar. And canning strawberries, sweet corn, green beans, and more was always a lot more fun with Grandma there to help as she had such interesting stories to tell.

We milked a herd of cows by hand. As a child, I always loved to watch the milking. I'd run to the house to get a glass and have Dad or Mom fill it with foaming, warm milk straight from the cow. As I grew, I'd race my siblings to see who could milk the fastest and most cows.

Now I have a family of my own and long to give them the good memories I had as a child. We do have a cow and a goat. The cow gives milk and cream which we use to make butter, ice cream, yogurt, and more. We grow as much of our own food as we can, and sometimes I have plenty to share.

FANNIE GLICK, Mount Victory, OH

Dairy

Surely the churning of milk
bringeth forth butter.

- Proverbs 30:33

Dairy Recipes:

Dairy most often refers to products made from the milk of cows, but sometimes goats and sheep are included. States have different laws about handling dairy between the farmer and the consumer. Some states don't prohibit it, and other states allow it if the farmer and buyer enter into a herd share contract. Check your local laws.

A large family that consumes a lot of milk can benefit from having a family cow. There is a lot to be learned about husbandry in caring for an animal that daily returns to you a product you can enjoy. Many people find raw milk (not pasteurized or homogenized) to be a superior source of vitamins and minerals. And, it makes the best homemade ice cream.

Best Yogurt

1 gallon skimmed milk
1 cup plain Greek yogurt
Sweetener of choice
Pinch of salt

In large saucepan, heat milk to 190 degrees. Take off heat and let cool to 120 degrees. Whisk in yogurt. Divide into wide-mouthed jars and screw on lids. Place jars in cooler chest and fill with hot water around 120 degrees. Close lid and let set undisturbed for 10 hours. Refrigerate jars overnight. Strain yogurt through a colander lined with cheesecloth (or new paint strainer bag) for 3 hours or until it looks nice and thick. Beat in sweetener of choice and pinch of salt and add fruit if desired.

Note: To use this like cream cheese, let yogurt drain for 12 hours then mix in just a pinch of salt.

Esther Troyer, Walhonding, OH

Cottage Cheese

3 quarts milk
½ cup vinegar
1 tablespoon salt
Cream or milk

In large saucepan, heat milk to boiling. Remove from heat and add vinegar. Pour into colander to drain off whey. Break curds into small curds and add salt and cream to taste.

Esther Troyer, Walhonding, OH

Marvel Cream Cheese

Make batch of homemade **yogurt**, but instead of refrigerating it, pour it through colander lined with triple thickness of cheesecloth. Catch whey in bowl under colander. Allow whey to drip for one minute then lift up four corners of the cheesecloth and tie them together. Hang bag and let whey drip for 6 to 8 hours. Remove from bag and store in the refrigerator until ready to use as cream cheese. One quart yogurt will make 6 to 8 ounces cream cheese.

Josephine Girod, Salem, IN

Spreading Cheese

1 gallon milk
1 cup vinegar
1 teaspoon baking soda
¼ cup butter
¼ cup heavy cream
1 teaspoon salt

In large saucepan, heat milk to 128 degrees. Remove from heat and add vinegar slowly while stirring. Let set for 1 hour then drain off whey through cheesecloth, letting it drip for 2 to 3 hours. Mix in baking soda. Let set for 1 hour, stirring occasionally. Return curds to saucepan or use double boiler over low heat and melt curds. Add butter, cream, and salt.

Esther Troyer, Walhonding, OH

Simple Delicious Cheese

2 gallons milk
2 cups vinegar
2 teaspoons baking soda
½ cup milk
4 tablespoons butter
2 teaspoons salt
2 tablespoons cheddar cheese powder (optional)

In saucepan, heat milk to 110 degrees. Add vinegar and let stand 10 minutes. Drain curds from whey through pillowcase and squeeze gently. Put in bowl and mix baking soda into curds. Let stand 1 hour. In saucepan, combine milk, butter, salt, and cheese powder and melt butter. Add cheese curds and mix well. Remove from heat and pack into container(s) and chill.

Lizzie N. Christner, Berne, IN

Simple Buttermilk Cheese

Allow jar of **buttermilk** to set at room temperature until sour. The more sour the buttermilk, the sharper the taste will be. Gently heat buttermilk to about 180 degrees. When buttermilk separates, remove from heat and pour into cloth-lined strainer. Knot ends of cloth and hang to finish draining. When cheese has drained to spreading consistency, add salt to taste. Store in cold place.

Miriam Hershberger, Apple Creek, OH

Homemade Butter

Put fresh **cream** into heavy bottomed saucepan or double boiler and stir constantly while heating to 145 to 150 degrees for 30 minutes. Increase temperature to 160 to 170 degrees for 5 minutes. Cool cream as rapidly as possible to 50 degrees or lower if you can. Let cream set for about 5 hours then churn at 50 to 60 degrees. Remove butter from churner and wash thoroughly in cold water. Add salt and work out as much water as possible. This makes very smooth, sweet butter and keeps longer than if made with raw cream.

Esther Troyer, Walhonding, OH

Whey

The whey you get from making cheese or Greek yogurt is very good to water your tomato plants or any other plants that need more calcium to prevent blossom-end rot.

Esther Troyer, Walhonding, OH

Cheese Spread

- 1 stick butter
- 6 cups milk
- 3 pounds Colby or Marble cheese
- 2 pounds Velveeta processed cheese

In saucepan, heat butter in milk but do not boil. In large bowl over hot water, melt together both cheeses. Add hot milk to melted cheese, stirring until smooth. Very good served on bread.

Mrs. Albert L. Yoder, Stanwood, MI

Cheddar Chowder

- 2 cups water
- 2 cups diced potatoes
- ½ cup diced carrots
- ½ cup diced celery
- ¼ cup chopped onion
- 1 teaspoon salt
- ¼ teaspoon pepper
- ¼ cup butter
- ¼ cup flour
- 2 to 3 cups milk
- 2 cups shredded cheese
- 1 cup cubed ham

In large kettle, combine water, potatoes, carrots, celery, onion, salt, and pepper. Boil 10 to 12 minutes. Meanwhile, in small saucepan, melt butter. Add flour and stir until smooth, cooking for 1 minute. Slowly add milk and cook until thickened. Add shredded cheese and stir until melted. When vegetables are tender, add cheese sauce and ham. Do not drain vegetables. Heat through.

Jerry and Ida Petersheim, Kenton, OH

Custard

This is so simple, and because the jars seal while cooking, it lasts a long time in the refrigerator. I often make a double batch since it doesn't last long in our home. I've used both jelly and pint jars, but jelly jars are perfect for lunch boxes.

1 quart cream
1 quart milk
8 eggs, beaten
1 cup maple syrup
1 teaspoon salt
Flavoring (cinnamon, coconut extract, shredded coconut, vanilla) (optional)

In bowl, mix all together and ladle into jars with lids. Set in kettle or canner with few inches of water. Bring to good boil and boil for 5 minutes. Turn off heat and let sit for 45 minutes with kettle lid on. Cool and enjoy.

Becky Fisher, Lancaster, PA

Baked Custard

1 cup sugar
1 cup brown sugar
4 eggs, separated
1 tablespoon plain gelatin
⅓ cup cold water
4 cups milk, heated
1 can evaporated milk

In bowl, cream together sugar, brown sugar, and egg yolks. In small bowl, soak gelatin in cold water. In another bowl, beat egg whites until stiff. Fold egg whites into creamed mixture. In saucepan, gently heat milk and evaporated milk to almost boiling. Add gelatin to milk and stir well. Add milk to creamed mixture, mixing well. Pour into 9x13-inch pan. Set it in larger pan with warm water. Bake at 450 degrees for 30 minutes or longer, until brown on top.

Mrs. David A. Yoder, Millersburg, OH

Pumpkin Custard

6 cups milk
6 eggs, separated
¾ cup maple syrup or honey
3 tablespoons tapioca starch
2 cups pumpkin puree
1 teaspoon salt
1 teaspoon cinnamon
1 teaspoon vanilla

In mixing bowl, mix together milk, egg yolks, maple syrup, tapioca starch, pumpkin puree, salt, cinnamon, and vanilla. In separate bowl, beat egg whites stiff. Fold into mixture. Pour into baking dish or ramekins or jars, set in pan with little water. Bake at 400 degrees for 10 minutes. Reduce heat to 350 degrees for 30 to 45 minutes.

Kevin Bontrager, Nappanee, IN

Just Right Custard Pie

2 eggs, separated
¾ cup sugar (half white and half brown)
2 level tablespoons flour
½ cup heavy cream
1 teaspoon vanilla
Pinch salt
1½ cups milk, heated
1 unbaked pie shell

In mixing bowl, beat egg yolks with sugar and flour. Add cream, vanilla, and salt. Stir in heated milk. In another bowl, beat egg whites until slightly stiffened and stir into mixture. Go slowly over top of mixture with egg beater to smooth out foam. Pour into unbaked pie shell. Bake at 400 degrees for 10 to 15 minutes. Reduce heat to 325 for 45 to 55 minutes or until nicely browned and set.

Clara Hershberger, Apple Creek, OH

Yogurt Pie

1¾ cups granola
2 tablespoons melted butter
3 tablespoons maple syrup
1 (8 ounce) package cream cheese
1 cup whipped topping
1½ cups yogurt
Fresh seasonal fruit

In bowl, mix granola, butter, and maple syrup. Press into 9-inch pie pan. Freeze until firm. In another bowl, blend cream cheese, whipped topping, and yogurt. Fill piecrust with mixture and top with fresh fruit.

Linda Fisher, Ronks, PA

Fruit Cream Pie

3 cups milk
1½ cups sugar
3 heaping tablespoons flour
1 cup heavy cream
Pinch salt
3 cups fresh fruit, sliced
1 unbaked pie shell

In saucepan, bring milk to boiling point. In bowl, blend sugar, flour, cream, and salt. Add to hot milk and bring to boiling point again. Cool. Add fresh fruit. Pour into unbaked pie shell. Bake at 400 degrees for 35 to 45 minutes.

Mrs. Johnny A. Troyer, Navarre, OH

Sour Cream Fruit Pie

2½ cups fruit filling of choice
1 (9 inch) unbaked pie shell
½ cup sugar
3 tablespoons flour
1 cup sour cream
1 (3 ounce) package cream cheese
½ cup flour
¼ cup sugar
2 tablespoons butter

Pour fruit filling in pie shell. In bowl, combine ½ cup sugar and 3 tablespoons flour. Add sour cream and cream cheese and blend well. Spread over fruit filling. In bowl, mix ½ cup flour, ¼ cup sugar, and butter until crumbly. Put over cream filling. Bake at 425 degrees for 15 minutes. Reduce heat to 350 degrees and bake for 25 minutes.

Delilah E. Schwartz, Berne, IN

Frozen Custard

4 cups heavy cream
2 cups skim milk
5 eggs
⅛ teaspoon salt
1 cup sugar
⅓ cup cornstarch
1 can sweetened condensed milk
⅓ cup maple syrup (no substitute)
2 tablespoons vanilla

In saucepan, combine cream and milk and bring to a boil. In bowl, beat eggs. Add salt, sugar, and cornstarch. Mix well. Stir into hot milk. Stir constantly until it thickens. Take off heat and stir in sweetened condensed milk, maple syrup, and vanilla. Strain mixture into ice cream freezer. Chill 1 to 2 days. Freeze according to ice cream freezer instructions. Taste and texture is like soft serve ice cream.

Mary Yoder, Mount Gilead, OH

Strawberry Ice Cream

3 quarts plus 1 cup milk, divided
3 cups sugar, divided
3 egg yolks
½ cup cornstarch
2 cups heavy cream
6 cups crushed strawberries

In saucepan, heat 3 quarts milk and 2 cups sugar to boiling point. In bowl, make paste of ¾ cup sugar, cornstarch, 1 cup milk, and egg yolks, beating until smooth. Stir into hot milk. Stir until just boiling. Remove from heat and cool. Before freezing according to freezer's instructions, add heavy cream and strawberries.

Julie Wengerd, Allensville, PA

Maple Walnut Ice Cream

We love homemade ice cream, and this is one of our favorites.

2½ cups maple syrup
3 cups whole milk
6 cups heavy cream
6 eggs
2 cups chopped walnuts (optional)

In heavy saucepan, cook syrup over high heat for 5 to 10 minutes until reduced by one fourth. Stir in milk and cream. Bring to slow boil. In large bowl, beat eggs and slowly add some hot cream. Whip mixture with a whisk. Pour into hot cream mixture and cook over low heat until mixture is slightly thick or temperature reaches at least 170 degrees. Do not boil. Chill for 3 hours. Freeze in 6-quart ice cream freezer.

Mrs. Susie Byler, Brockway, PA

Fruits

Eat an apple, save the core, plant the seeds and raise some more.

– Amish Saying

Fruit Recipes:

Fruits are a sweet gift from nature. Whether from a wild bramble or a well-pruned tree, fruit is worth picking and preserving. A farm that sells fruit by the pound or the bushel can be found in most communities. Many farms are also available for a pick-your-own experience. Other farms will process their fruit into a yummy jam, pie filling, cider, or apple cider vinegar you can buy.

APPLES

BERRIES

GRAPES

PEACHES

OTHER FRUITS

Blessed of the LORD is his land,
With the precious things of
heaven, with the dew,
And the deep lying beneath,
With the precious fruits of the sun,
With the precious produce of the months.

– DUETERONOMY 33:13-14 NKJV

Apples

Mulled Cider

1 gallon fresh **apple cider**
¼ cup honey or ½ cup brown sugar
1 tablespoon cinnamon
1 tablespoon lemon juice
2 tablespoons whole cloves

In saucepan, combine all ingredients and simmer for 20 minutes. Serve hot.

Jemima Wengerd, Salem, IN

Apple Salad

2 cups whipping cream
½ cup honey
½ cup peanut butter
2 to 2½ cups diced **apples**

In bowl, whip cream to peak. Mix in honey and peanut butter. Fold in apples.

Harvey Byler Family, Fredericktown, OH

Apple Fritters

This recipe comes from my grandma. Dip them in warm maple syrup. Yum!

1 cup flour
1½ teaspoons baking powder
3 tablespoons powdered sugar
¼ teaspoon salt
½ cup milk
1 egg, well beaten
2 medium **apples**
Coconut oil

In bowl, mix flour, baking powder, powdered sugar, and salt. Gradually add milk and egg. Pare, core, and cut apples in eighths. Slice thinly and stir into batter. Drop by spoonful into hot oil and fry until golden brown and crisp.

Anna Swartzentruber, West Salem, OH

Apple Dumplings

2 cups flour
½ cup water
1 teaspoon salt
⅔ cup shortening
6 apples peeled and cored
¼ cup sugar
1 tablespoon cinnamon
6 teaspoons butter

In bowl, mix flour, water, salt, and shortening until it comes together. Roll dough out into rectangle and cut 6 squares. Place an apple on each square. In small bowl, mix sugar and cinnamon. Divided over apples. Top each apple with 1 teaspoon butter. Bring dough up sides of apples and press edges to seal. Place in 9x13-inch pan.

Syrup:

1 cup brown sugar
2 cups water
¼ cup butter
1 tablespoon cinnamon

In saucepan, mix all ingredients together and heat until dissolved. Pour over apples in pan. Bake at 350 degrees for 45 minutes. Serve warm with milk or vanilla ice cream.

Laura Troyer, Blanchard, MI

Apple Crisp

4 cups chopped apples
½ cup sugar
1 tablespoon flour
2 teaspoons cinnamon
½ teaspoon nutmeg or to taste
¼ cup melted butter
¾ cup quick oats
¼ cup sifted flour
¼ cup sugar
¼ cup brown sugar

In bowl, combine apples, ½ cup sugar, and 1 tablespoon flour. Put in baking dish and sprinkle with cinnamon and nutmeg. In another bowl, combine butter, oats, sifted flour, ¼ cup sugar, and brown sugar. Sprinkle on top of apples. Bake at 375 degrees for 45 minutes or until apples are soft.

Sam and Edna Eicher, Rockford, OH

Autumn Apple Cake with Caramel Icing

4 cups peeled and chopped apples
1 cup sugar
2 eggs, beaten
½ cup butter, melted
2 cups unbleached flour
2 teaspoons baking soda
¾ teaspoon salt
1 teaspoon cinnamon
¼ teaspoon ground ginger
¼ teaspoon ground nutmeg
1 cup chopped pecans

In mixing bowl, combine apples and sugar; let stand for few minutes or until apples release juices. Mix in eggs and melted butter. In another bowl, combine flour, baking soda, salt, cinnamon, ginger, nutmeg, and pecans. Add mixture to apples and mix until combined. Spread into greased 9x13-inch pan. Bake at 325 degrees for 35 minutes or until cake tester or toothpick inserted in center comes out clean.

Caramel icing:

¼ cup butter
⅓ cup brown sugar
⅛ teaspoon salt
2 tablespoons milk
1 cup powdered sugar
½ teaspoon vanilla

In small saucepan, melt butter. Stir in brown sugar and salt. Cook, stirring constantly, until sugar melts. Add milk and bring to boil. Pour into mixing bowl and cool for 10 minutes. After cooling, stir in powdered sugar and vanilla, whisking until smooth. Spread over warm cake.

Saloma Zook, Fredericksburg, OH

Apple Pie Bars

Dough:

- 4 cups flour
- 1 teaspoon baking powder
- 4 egg yolks
- 8 to 10 teaspoons cold water
- 1 teaspoon salt
- 1 cup shortening
- 2 tablespoons lemon juice

In bowl, work all ingredients together to form dough ball. Divide in half. Roll one half dough out into 12x17-inch rectangle. Transfer to ungreased 10x15-inch baking pan. Press dough onto bottom and up sides of pan. Trim dough even with top edge of pan.

Filling:

- 7 cups peeled, chopped apples
- ¼ cup flour
- Dash ground nutmeg
- 2 cups sugar
- 2 teaspoons cinnamon

In bowl, combine all ingredients and spread over crust. Roll out remaining dough to fit top of pan. Place over filling and pinch along edges to seal. Cut vent slits into top of crust. Bake at 375 degrees for 45 to 50 minutes or until filling is bubbly.

Glaze

- 1 cup powdered sugar
- 1 tablespoon lemon juice
- 1 tablespoon milk

In small bowl, mix all ingredients until smooth. Drizzle over bars.

Sadie Bender, Meyersdale, PA

Glazed Apple Cookies

2½ cups brown sugar
1 cup lard
2 eggs
½ cup milk
4 cups flour
1 teaspoon ground clove
1 teaspoon cinnamon
2 teaspoons baking soda
2 cups chopped **apples**

In mixing bowl, cream brown sugar and lard. Beat in eggs and milk. Stir in flour, clove, cinnamon, and baking soda. Fold in apples. Drop by spoonful onto baking sheets and bake at 375 degrees for 10 minutes. Glaze while still warm.

Glaze:

2 cups powdered sugar
1 tablespoon butter
3 tablespoons milk
Maple flavoring

In bowl, blend powdered sugar, butter, and milk until smooth. Add maple flavoring to taste. Spread over warm cookies.

Sadie D. Byler, Brookville, PA

Apple Butter

- 4 gallons apples, unpeeled and quartered (Jonathan are best)
- 8 pounds organic raw cane sugar (can reduce)
- 3 tablespoons cinnamon
- ½ tablespoon nutmeg
- ¼ teaspoon ground clove

Place apples in heavy kettle with tight lid. Withhold about 1 cup of sugar then pour remaining sugar over apples. Let stand, covered, overnight to form juice. Bring apples slowly to boil and simmer 3 hours. Don't open lid or stir during entire cooking time. Put apples through a Victoria strainer like you would for applesauce. Mix 1 cup sugar with cinnamon, nutmeg, and clove. Mix well into strained apples. Ladle into canning jars and cold pack for 20 minutes. Yields 25 pints.

Simon and Ida Miller, Clark, MO

Apple Pie Filling

6 cups sugar
5 heaping tablespoons instant Clear Jel (cornstarch)
1 teaspoon cinnamon
Pinch salt
16 cups chopped apples
½ cup lemon juice
3 to 4 cups water

In small bowl, mix sugar, Clear Jel, cinnamon, and salt and pour over apples, mixing until coated. In bowl, mix lemon juice and water. Stir into apples. Let stand 10 minutes. Ladle into canning jars and cold pack for 10 minutes to seal.

Marie Detweiler, Smicksburg, PA

Applescotch Pie

5 cups sliced apples
1 cup brown sugar
¼ cup water
1 tablespoon lemon juice
¼ cup flour
2 tablespoons sugar
¾ tablespoon salt
3 tablespoons butter
1 teaspoon vanilla
1 unbaked pie shell

In 2-quart saucepan over low heat, combine apples, brown sugar, water, and lemon juice and cook uncovered until tender (7 to 8 minutes). Stir gently occasionally. In small bowl, mix flour and sugar. Add to apples and cook until thickened. Remove from heat and add salt, butter, and vanilla. Pour into pie shell.

Topping:

¾ cup flour
½ cup brown sugar
⅓ cup butter, softened

Mix all ingredients together and spread on top of apple filling. Bake at 375 degrees for 45 to 50 minutes.

Laura Troyer, Blanchard, MI

No Sugar Apple Pie

1 cup raisins
½ cup water
4 cups sliced apples
3 tablespoons minute tapioca
⅓ cup water
¼ teaspoon salt
½ teaspoon cinnamon
1 unbaked pie crust

In saucepan, cook raisins in ½ cup water for 5 minutes. Blend raisins until smooth and mix with apples. Add tapioca, ⅓ cup water, salt, and cinnamon. Pour into pie crust. Bake at 425 degrees for 10 minutes. Reduce heat to 350 degrees and bake for 30 to 35 minutes.

Ruby E. Schwartz, Geneva, IN

Berries

Fresh Strawberry Lemonade

This drink tastes especially good right after you are done mowing the lawn on a really warm day.

1 cup evaporated cane sugar
1 cup water
3 cups fresh sliced strawberries, divided
1½ cups fresh lemon juice (about 6 lemons)
6 cups cold water
Ice
Lemon slices for garnish (optional)

In a small saucepan, bring sugar and 1 cup water to a boil. Remove from heat and let cool to room temperature. Place 2 cups strawberries in food processor or blender and process until smooth. Pour pureed strawberries into sugar water. Add lemon juice and stir well. Pour into a large pitcher. Add 6 cups cold water and ice and stir well. Pour into individual glasses. Top with reserved 1 cup of sliced strawberries and slices of lemon. Serves 6 to 8.

Mervin and Lorene Miller, Whittemore, MI
Anna Swartzentruber, West Salem, OH

Strawberry Soup

Fresh strawberries, diced
Sugar
Bread, cubed
Milk

In bowl, mix strawberries with sugar to your taste. Add as much bread as you like. Cover with milk as soupy as you like. This is very delicious served with fried potatoes.

Salome B. Schwartz, Monroe, IN

Mixed Berry Smoothie

1 cup frozen strawberries
½ cup frozen blueberries
1 frozen banana
¾ cup yogurt
Few drops liquid stevia

In blender, blend strawberries, blueberries, banana, yogurt, and few drops stevia. If your fruit isn't frozen, add some ice cubes. Blend until smooth.

Lucinda Schwartz, Berne, IN

Anna Swartzentruber, West Salem, OH

Mary Yoder, Mount Gilead, OH

Best Ever Smoothie Bowls

A refreshing summer snack and a great way to use up frozen fruit.

1¼ cups frozen raspberries
1½ cups frozen blueberries
1½ cups frozen strawberries
1 pint canned peaches
2 tablespoons honey
Garnish: melted peanut butter, granola, fresh berries, honey, chocolate chips, etc.

In blender, blend raspberries, blueberries, strawberries, peaches, and honey while fruit is still frozen. Spoon into bowls about ¾ way full. Garnish as desired. It is good to drizzle melted peanut butter and top with granola and fresh fruit. Or drizzle with honey and sprinkle with chocolate chips. Serve immediately. Makes about 4 servings.

Marlene Stoltzfus, Gap, PA

Fresh Berry Medley

- 1 cup sparkling wine or white grape juice
- ½ cup sugar
- ⅛ teaspoon salt
- 1½ teaspoons lemon zest
- 1 tablespoon lemon juice
- ½ teaspoon vanilla
- 8 cups mixed fresh berries (strawberries, raspberries, blueberries)
- Fresh mint (optional)

In saucepan, combine sparkling wine, sugar, salt, lemon zest, lemon juice, and vanilla. Heat to boiling. Refrigerate. In medium bowl, toss berries with chilled sauce. Refrigerate 1 to 2 hours before serving. Garnish with fresh mint, if desired.

Saloma Zook, Fredericksburg, OH

Favorite Blueberry Muffins

3 cups flour
4 teaspoons baking powder
1 teaspoon salt
1 cup sugar
2 eggs, beaten
1 cup milk
½ cup canola oil
2 cups blueberries

In bowl, blend flour, baking powder, salt, and sugar. In another bowl, beat eggs with milk and oil. Combine into dry mixture, only until moistened. Stir in blueberries. Bake in greased muffin pans at 375 for 20 to 25 minutes. Remove from oven and let cool several minutes. Remove from pan.

Topping:

Butter
Cinnamon
Sugar

Melt butter in one bowl and in another blend cinnamon and sugar to your taste. Dip muffin tops in butter then into cinnamon-sugar mixture.

Mrs. Albert L. Yoder, Stanwood, MI

Strawberry-Rhubarb Muffins

1¾ cups flour
½ cup sugar
2½ teaspoons baking powder
½ teaspoon salt
1 egg, beaten
¾ cup milk
½ cup oil
¾ cup minced rhubarb
½ cup sliced strawberries
6 strawberries cut in half
Additional sugar for topping

In bowl, mix flour, sugar, baking powder, and salt. In another bowl, combine egg, milk, and oil. Stir into flour mixture with fork until just moistened. Fold in rhubarb and sliced strawberries. Fill 12 well-greased or lined muffin cups ⅔ full. Gently press half strawberry into top of each muffin. Sprinkle tops generously with sugar. Bake at 400 degrees for 20 to 25 minutes. Remove from pan and cool on racks. Yields 12 muffins.

Lizzie Ann Swartzentruber, Newcomerstown, OH

Blueberry Lemon Bread

½ cup butter
1⅓ cups sugar
2 teaspoons baking powder
½ teaspoon salt
2 eggs
2 cups flour
½ cup milk
¼ cup lemon juice
1½ cups **blueberries,** fresh or frozen
⅓ cup sugar

In mixing bowl, beat together butter and 1⅓ cups sugar. Add baking powder and salt, mixing well. Beat in eggs. Add flour and mix well. Stir in milk and lemon juice. Gently stir in blueberries. Pour into 1 large or 2 small greased loaf pans. Bake at 350 degrees for 1 hour. In small bowl, blend lemon juice with ⅓ cup sugar until dissolved. When bread is done, prick top with fork and brush with mixture. Delicious served warm with ice cream.

Mary Yoder, Mount Gilead, OH

Blueberry Pudding Cake

1½ cups sugar, divided
4 tablespoons melted butter, divided
1 egg
1 cup buttermilk
½ teaspoon baking soda
1 teaspoon baking powder
½ teaspoon salt
2 cups flour
1 cup fresh **blueberries**

In mixing bowl, combine 1 cup sugar and 2 tablespoons melted butter. Add egg and buttermilk, mixing well. Add baking soda, baking powder, salt, and flour. Stir in blueberries. Pour into 9x13-inch pan. In small bowl, combine 2 tablespoons melted butter and ½ cup sugar. Sprinkle over cake batter. Bake at 350 degrees for 45 minutes.

Sauce:

½ cup sugar
½ cup butter
½ cup heavy cream
1 teaspoon vanilla

In saucepan, combine sugar, butter, and cream. Bring to boil and boil for 1 minute. Remove from heat and add vanilla. Serve cake with warm sauce.

Lori Miller, Middlefield, OH

Raspberry Cream Pops

1 cup fresh or frozen **raspberries** or other fruit
1 (3 ounce) package instant vanilla pudding
1 cup cold milk
¼ cup condensed milk
¼ cup yogurt
1 cup whipped topping

Put all ingredients in blender and blend until smooth. Pour into popsicle molds and freeze.

Esther Detweiler, Mechanicstown, OH

Fresh Icehouse Strawberries

Pick **strawberries** early in the morning while they are still cool. Work them up immediately, making sure to cut out all bad spots completely. Put through salsa maker or mash fine. Make sure jars and plastic lids are sterile and cool. Fill jars to brim so no air remains. Add no sweeteners. Screw on tight-fitting plastic lids. Store in icehouse inside large totes or milk cans with water covering jars so no air can get inside. Keep ice in totes. These should still taste fresh until February. Sweetener can be added when opening the jars, if desired.

Simon and Ida Miller, Clark, MO

We do this also with blueberries.

Daniel and Mary Shetler, Homer, MI

Strawberry Jam

5 cups crushed strawberries
7 cups sugar
½ cup Dutch Jel or Sure-Jell

Combine all ingredients in saucepan and bring to boil for 15 minutes. Ladle into jelly jars and seal. Place in hot water bath for 5 minutes.

Marie Detweiler, Smicksburg, PA

Easy Freezer Jam

This recipe was handed down from my great-aunt and requires less sugar than other jams.

4 cups mashed berries of choice
2 boxes or ⅔ cup pectin
5 to 6 cups sugar

In bowl, stir berries and pectin together. Let sit 30 to 60 minutes. Mix in sugar. Let sit, but stir occasionally for 15 minutes. Put into freezer containers and freeze.

Titus and Edna Miller, Lawrence, MI

Blueberry Pie Filling

10 cups water
5 cups sugar
1½ cups Perma Flo
1 tablespoon salt
2 tablespoons lemon juice
8 to 10 cups blueberries

In kettle, cook water and sugar until sugar dissolves. Dissolve Perma Flo in a little water and add to sugar water. Bring to boil while stirring. Remove from heat and add salt and lemon juice, mixing well. Add blueberries. Ladle into jars and cold pack for 10 minutes to seal. The longer you wait to use it, the deeper the color will get.

Barbara Miller, Big Prairie, OH

Raspberry Pie Filling

5 cups raspberries
4 cups water
6 cups sugar
4 tablespoons butter
Pinch salt
2 cups Perma-Flo
½ cup red raspberry gelatin
½ cup black raspberry gelatin

In kettle, cook raspberries in water to release juices. Strain pulp. To juice, add enough water to equal 10 cups. In kettle, combine raspberry juice, sugar, butter, and salt. Bring to boil. Dissolve Perma Flo in little water and add to boiling juice, stirring to thicken. Remove from heat and add gelatins. Ladle into jars and cold pack for 10 minutes to seal.

Barbara Miller, Big Prairie, OH

Grape Salad

1 (8 ounces) package cream cheese
1½ cups powdered sugar
1 teaspoon lemon juice
1 (8 ounce) carton sour cream
1 (8 ounce) carton whipped topping
4 pounds grapes

In bowl, blend cream cheese and powdered sugar until smooth. Fold in lemon juice, sour cream, and whipped topping. Add grapes, stirring to coat. Note: You can substitute or add other fruits like blueberries, chopped apples, or segmented oranges.

Delilah Christner, Decatur, IN

Ruben and Ruth Schwartz, Connersville, IN

Grape Juice

2 cups fresh, cleaned grapes
1 cup sugar

In 2-quart/half gallon canning jar, place grapes and sugar then fill jar with hot water. Stir until sugar is dissolved. Seal jar in hot water bath until water comes to rolling boil. Let set a few weeks before using. This is not a concentrate. Drain grapes before serving juice.

Anna M. Weaver, Mertztown, PA

Grape Juice Concentrate

15 cups grapes
9 cups water
3½ cups sugar

In kettle, bring grapes and water to the boiling point. Boil 5 minutes. Drain through colander. Add sugar to juice and return to boil. Ladle into canning jars. Cold pack 10 minutes to seal. When opening to use, add water to taste. You can also thicken juice with Clear Jel and a little water for pie filling.

Mrs. Joseph Miller, Navarre, OH

Grape Pie Filling

Grapes
2 cups water
4 cups sugar
½ teaspoon salt
2⅔ cups Perma Flo
2 cups water

Fill 6-quart saucepan ¾ full with grapes then cover with water. Boil for 10 minutes. Strain juice from pulp. Place 3 quarts juice with 2 cups water in 6-quart saucepan. When hot, add sugar and salt. Dissolve Perma Flo in 2 cups water. Add to hot juice. Bring to boil. Ladle into quart canning jars. Seal in hot water bath for 10 minutes. Makes 4 quarts.

Katie Yoder, Sugarcreek, OH

Peaches

Peach Crunch

4 cups chopped peaches
1 tablespoon honey
1 tablespoon flour
1 cup flour
2 teaspoons baking powder
½ teaspoon salt
2 tablespoons butter
¾ cup honey
1 egg, beaten

Mix peaches, 1 tablespoon honey, and 1 tablespoon flour. Place in 9x9-inch pan. In bowl, mix 1 cup flour, baking powder, salt, butter, ¾ cup honey, and egg. Cover peaches with mixture. Bake at 400 degrees 20 to 30 minutes until browned.

Esther Troyer, Walhonding, OH

Peaches and Cream Bars

3 cups flour
1½ cups sugar
¼ teaspoon salt
1½ cups unsalted butter, chilled
4 large eggs
2 cups sugar
1 cup sour cream
¾ cup flour
Pinch of salt
2 pounds peaches, sliced thinly

In mixing bowl, blend 3 cups flour, 1½ cups sugar, and salt. Cut in butter and mix until appears crumbly. Remove 1½ cups of mixture; set aside. Press remaining mixture into a 9x13-inch pan and bake at 350 degrees for 12 to 15 minutes. Let cool for 10 minutes. In large bowl, whisk eggs with 2 cups sugar. Add sour cream, ¾ cup flour, and salt. Fold in peaches and spread over crust. Bake at 350 degrees for 45 to 50 minutes until top is slightly browned and filling is set. Cool for an hour before cutting into bars.

Mary A. Swartzentruber, Dalton, OH

Other Fruits

Fruit Cocktail to Can

1 bushel **pears**, peeled and chunked
1 bushel **peaches**, peeled and chunked
2 gallons pineapple tidbits
10 pounds white **grapes**, halved
Maraschino cherries, halved
Sugar
Water

Mix pears, peaches, pineapple, grapes, and cherries. In saucepan, dissolve sugar in water using the chart below to your preferred taste. Mix syrup into fruit. Ladle into quart canning jars. Cold pack 15 minutes. Makes 50 quarts.

Syrup for Canning Fruit:

Heavy syrup – 1 cup sugar to 1 cup water
Medium syrup – 1 cup sugar to 2 cups water
Light syrup – 1 cup sugar to 3 to 4 cups water

Mary Yoder, Mount Gilead, OH

Persimmon Pudding

1½ cups **persimmons**
3 cups milk, divided
1 cup organic raw sugar
2 scant cups flour (Turkey Red)
Pinch salt
½ teaspoon baking soda
1 teaspoon baking powder
1 teaspoon cinnamon
2 large eggs, beaten well
½ cup butter, melted

In mixing bowl, mix persimmons, 1 cup milk, sugar, flour, salt, baking soda, baking powder, and cinnamon; mix well. Add remaining 2 cups milk and eggs. Mix well. Stir in melted butter. Pour into greased 9x13-inch baking dish. Bake at 350 degrees for 30 to 40 minutes. Do not overbake.

Simon and Ida Miller, Clark, MO

Watermelon Breeze

This is a fresh and low-calorie summer drink.

3 to 4 cups cubed **watermelon**, chilled
1 cup water
Squeeze of fresh lime
Ice cubes

Put all ingredients in blender and blend until smooth. Pour into glasses and add ice cubes. Serves 2.

Leah D. L. Coblentz, Portland, IN
Miriam Hershberger, Apple Creek, OH
Anna Swartzentruber, West Salem, OH
Mary Yoder, Mount Gilead, OH

Ethel Blackwell's Plum Pie

4 cups sliced plums or concord grapes
1 tablespoon lemon juice
½ cup sugar
¼ cup flour
¼ teaspoon salt
¼ teaspoon cinnamon
1 (9 inch) unbaked pie shell

In mixing bowl, sprinkle plums with lemon juice. In another bowl, combine sugar, flour, salt and cinnamon. Add to plums; toss gently to coat. Pour into pie shell. Prepare topping.

Topping:

½ cup sugar
¼ cup flour
¼ teaspoon cinnamon
¼ teaspoon nutmeg
3 tablespoons butter

In a bowl, blend sugar, flour, cinnamon, and nutmeg. Work in butter until crumbly. Sprinkle over filling. Bake at 375 degrees for 50 to 60 minutes until filling is bubbly.

MaryAnn Weaver, Howard, OH

Ground Cherry Pie

This was my grandmother's recipe and the best I've ever eaten.

2 cups ground cherries
1 cup brown sugar
1 tablespoon lemon juice
¼ teaspoon salt
2 to 3 tablespoons Clear Jel
1 tablespoon butter
1 unbaked pie shell with top

In saucepan, place cherries in just enough water to cover. Add brown sugar, lemon juice, and salt. Bring to boil. Thicken with Clear Jel to your liking. Boil on low heat for 2 minutes. Remove from heat and add butter. Pour into unbaked pie shell. Top with crust, pinching to seal and cutting some vents. Bake at 450 degrees for 10 minutes, then reduce heat to 350 degrees and bake 40 minutes or until golden brown.

Raymond and Miriam Troyer, Blanchard, MI

Grains, Nuts, and Seeds

"But when the grain ripens, immediately he puts in the sickle, because the harvest has come."

~ Mark 4:29 NKJV

Grains, Nuts & Seeds Recipes:

Some small farms cultivate crops of grains like oats and spelt, nuts like walnuts, seeds like sunflower, and corn for cornmeal and popcorn that they will sell. Look for these farmers at local markets to also offer them in products like bread and granola.

Toasted Oats

12 cups oatmeal
4 teaspoons cinnamon
2 cups brown sugar
2 cups butter, melted

In bowl, mix all ingredients well. Spread in roasting pans. Bake at 300 degrees for approximately 1½ hours, stirring every 20 minutes. Good to eat as cereal or in yogurt parfait.

Mrs. David B. Schwartz, Salem, IN

Spelt Berries

Sometimes I serve **spelt berries** we grow as a side dish instead of rice or potatoes. First, rinse them under running water to remove any dirt and debris. Next, soak spelt in water for 8 hours or overnight. Drain and rinse. In saucepan, add 3 parts water to each 1 part spelt berries. Bring to boil and simmer on low for about 1 hour. Season as desired.

Ora Borntreger, Campbellsburg, IN

Cereal Cake

2 cups quick oats
1 cup cornmeal
2 cups farina or whole wheat or graham flour
1 cup sugar
2 teaspoons baking powder
1 teaspoon baking soda
1 teaspoon salt
1 cup softened butter or oil
2 cups milk

In bowl, mix oats, cornmeal, farina, sugar, baking powder, baking soda, and salt. (You can prep this part the night before baking.) Add butter and milk, stirring until mixed. Pour into greased 9x13-inch pan. Bake at 350 degrees for 30 to 40 minutes until done.

Sylvia Miller, Middlefield, OH

Baked Oatmeal

Fruit
¼ cup honey
½ cup melted butter
2 eggs, beaten
3 cups **oatmeal** or 2½ cups oatmeal and ½ cup crushed wheat flour
1 teaspoon baking powder
1 teaspoon baking soda
½ teaspoon salt
1 cup milk

Put your favorite fruit, like blueberries, on the bottom of 9x13-inch pan. Place in 350-degree oven to heat while you prepare batter. In bowl, mix honey, butter, eggs, oatmeal, baking powder, baking soda, salt, and milk. Pour over fruit. Bake at 350 degrees for 30 minutes.

Ruth Wengerd, Burton, OH

Berry Baked Oatmeal

1 cup blueberries or blackberries
½ cup melted butter
1 cup maple syrup or brown sugar
2 eggs
3 cups **oatmeal**
2 teaspoons baking powder
1 teaspoon salt
1 teaspoon cinnamon
1 cup milk

Scatter berries in 8x8-inch baking dish. In mixing bowl, blend butter, maple syrup, eggs, oatmeal, baking powder, salt, cinnamon, and milk. Pour over berries. Refrigerate overnight. Bake at 350 degrees for 40 minutes. Serve with milk or yogurt.

Rebecca Glick, Bird-in-Hand, PA

Baked Pumpkin Oatmeal

2 cups **old-fashioned oatmeal**
¼ cup brown sugar
1 teaspoon cinnamon
½ teaspoon nutmeg
1 teaspoon baking powder
1 cup milk
1 teaspoon vanilla
1 cup pureed pumpkin
1 tablespoon oil
1 egg, beaten

In bowl, combine oatmeal, brown sugar, cinnamon, nutmeg, and baking powder. In another bowl, mix milk, vanilla, pumpkin, oil, and egg. Add mixture to oat mixture. Stir and pour into greased 1½ quart baking dish. Bake at 375 degrees for 20 minutes. Serve warm.

Ruby Joann Miller, Auburn, KY

Spelt Pancakes

On our farm, we grow, clean, grind, and sell spelt.

1¼ cups **spelt flour**
1 tablespoon baking powder
½ teaspoon salt
1 tablespoon sugar
2 tablespoons olive oil
1 cup milk
1 egg

In bowl, mix all ingredients and let sit a few minutes to allow spelt time to absorb some of the moisture. Pour ¼ cup of batter onto hot griddle or skillet. Flip when edges start to curl up or bottom is golden brown.

Ora Borntreger, Campbellsburg, IN

Cornmeal Mush

1 cup **cornmeal**
1 teaspoon salt
1 cup cold water
3 cups boiling water

Mix cornmeal, salt, and cold water. In kettle, boil 3 cups water and mix in cornmeal. Cook over low heat until thickened, stirring often. Then cook on low for 15 minutes. Pour into loaf pan and cool thoroughly. Slice and fry in oil. Serve with maple syrup.

Susan Schwartz, Berne, IN

Homemade Scrapple

4 quarts meat broth
4 cups cornmeal
1 cup quick oats
1 cup flour
1 tablespoon pepper
1 tablespoon salt
¼ teaspoon cayenne powder
¼ teaspoon hickory smoke salt
½ teaspoon ground fennel
1 teaspoon chicken base
1 quart canned loose sausage

In bowl, mix meat broth, cornmeal, oats, and flour. Set in cool place for 6 to 8 hours. Place mixture in kettle, and add pepper, salt, cayenne powder, hickory smoke salt, fennel, chicken base, and sausage. Cook and stir until boiling. Cover and turn to lowest heat and simmer 30 minutes. Pour into loaf pans to cool. Refrigerate up to 6 days. For longer storage, freeze. Slice and fry in cast-iron skillet with hot lard. If using fresh meat and broth, add an extra 1 tablespoon salt.

Susan Troyer, East Rochester, OH

Buttery Cornbread

⅔ cup butter, softened
⅔ cup sugar
3 eggs
1⅔ cups milk
2⅓ cups flour
1 cup cornmeal
4½ teaspoons baking powder
1 teaspoon salt

In mixing bowl, cream butter and sugar. In small bowl, combine eggs and milk. In another mixing bowl, combine flour, cornmeal, baking powder, and salt. Alternately add dry mixture and egg mixture to creamed mixture. Pour into greased 9x13-inch pan. Bake at 400 degrees for 22 to 27 minutes or until toothpick inserted in center comes out clean. Cut into squares and serve warm. Yields 12 to 15 servings.

Judith Miller, Fredericktown, OH

Honey Oatmeal Bread

4 tablespoons yeast
1½ cups warm water
½ cup honey
2 cups oatmeal
1 teaspoon salt
⅔ cup butter
4 eggs
1½ cups water
9 to 10 cups flour

In bowl, mix yeast and warm water and let sit about 5 minutes. Add honey, oatmeal, salt, butter, eggs, and water. Mix in flour and knead well. Allow to rise and double in size. Punch dough down and shape into 4 loaves. Place into greased pans and let rise. Bake at 350 degrees for 30 minutes. Makes 4 (1½ pound) loaves.

Harvey Byler Family, Fredericktown, OH

Granola Bars

½ cup butter, melted
½ cup honey
¼ cup molasses
⅔ cup peanut butter
3 cups quick oats
½ cup carob chips or chocolate chips
½ cup sunflower seeds
½ cup shredded coconut

In mixing bowl, blend butter, honey, molasses, and peanut butter. Mix in oats, carob chips, sunflower seeds, and coconut. Pour into greased 9x13-inch pan. Bake at 350 degrees for 20 minutes. Cut into bars.

Grace Zimmerman, Shiloh, OH

Chunky Oatmeal Bars

¾ cup butter, softened
1 cup packed brown sugar
2 teaspoons vanilla
1 cup flour
2 tablespoons unsweetened cocoa powder
1½ teaspoons baking powder
¼ teaspoon salt
¼ cup water
1 to 1¼ cups quick oats
1 (12 ounce) package semisweet chocolate chunks

In mixing bowl, cream butter with brown sugar until smooth. Beat in vanilla until light in color. In a small bowl, combine flour, cocoa, baking powder, and salt. Blend dry mixture into creamed mixture. Add water. Stir in oats and chocolate chunks. Put into lightly greased 9-inch square pan. Bake at 375 degrees for 25 to 30 minutes.

Grace Zimmerman, Shiloh, OH

Butter Pecan Sauce

½ cup butter
1 cup pecan pieces
1 cup brown sugar
½ cup heavy whipping cream
½ cup corn syrup
½ teaspoon salt

In saucepan, melt butter. Add pecans and stir until butter starts to brown. Stir in brown sugar, cream, corn syrup, and salt. Cook gently until sugar is dissolved. Serve over ice cream, cake, or whatever you wish.

Susan Gingerich, Dalton, OH

Oatmeal Pie Crust

1½ cups **oatmeal**
½ cup butter, melted
½ cup flour

Mix all ingredients well and press into pie pan. Bake at 350 degrees for 20 minutes. The mixture can also be baked in 9x9 baking pan for dessert crust.

Kevin Bontrager, Nappanee, IN

Pecan Pie Cobbler

½ cup butter, melted
1⅛ cups flour
¾ cup sugar
1 tablespoon baking powder
¼ teaspoon salt
⅔ cup milk
1 teaspoon vanilla
1½ cups chopped **pecans**
1 cup brown sugar
1½ cups boiling water

Pour butter into 9x13-inch pan. In bowl, mix flour, sugar, baking powder, and salt. Stir in milk and vanilla. Put mixture on top of butter. Sprinkle with pecans and brown sugar. Pour boiling water over all. Bake at 350 degrees for 30 to 35 minutes until set. Serve with ice cream.

Sharon Miller, Auburn, KY

Spiced Nuts

1 egg white
¼ cup sugar
1 tablespoon cinnamon or pumpkin pie spice
1 cup **nut meats** (walnut, pecan, etc)

Beat egg white until frothy. Add sugar, cinnamon, and nuts, mixing well to coat nuts. Put on baking sheet and bake at 250 degrees for 20 to 30 minutes, stirring frequently, until dry and crusty and darkened.

Elizabeth Kinsinger, Meyersdale, PA

Cracker Jacks

3 gallons **popped corn**
1½ cups sorghum molasses
2½ cups organic raw sugar
1½ teaspoons apple cider vinegar
1½ tablespoons butter
⅓ teaspoon baking soda

Butter 16-quart bowl, add popcorn and set aside. In saucepan, combine molasses, sugar, vinegar, and butter. Bring to boil to 265 degrees until syrup hardens in cold water. Add baking soda and stir briskly. Pour over popcorn and stir until well coated. Spread onto greased cookie sheets and bake at 250 degrees for 10 minutes. Cool to harden before serving. If there are any leftovers, store in airtight containers.

Simon and Ida Miller, Clark, MO

Meat and Eggs

And you shall rejoice in your feast,
you and your son and your daughter,
your male servant and your female servant
and the Levite, the stranger and the fatherless
and the widow, who are within your gates.

- Deuteronomy 16:14 NKJV

Meat and Egg Recipes:

When you buy your meat from a small local farm, you can be fairly certain that the animal was treated well in life and respected for the food it produces. Farmers are known for staying up nights worrying about a cow about to calve or a storm coming through that might endanger the herd or flock. The farmer you buy direct from will most likely welcome you on a tour of the farm and let you meet some of the stock.

BEEF

EGGS

FISH

PORK

POULTRY

Beef

Cheeseburger Salad

2 sesame hamburger buns
1 small onion
¾ pound ground beef
Salt and pepper to taste
½ cup chopped dill pickles
¾ cup ketchup
½ cup mayonnaise
1 tablespoon mustard
8 cups chopped lettuce
1 cup shredded cheese
2 tomatoes, sliced or chopped

Cut buns into cubes and brown in dry skillet. Cut onion in half. Slice half and chop the other half. In skillet, brown beef and season with salt and pepper to taste; drain. Add chopped onion, pickles, ketchup, mayonnaise, and mustard. Arrange lettuce on platter. Top with beef mixture, cheese, bread cubes, sliced onion, and tomatoes. Serve while beef is still warm.

Katie Kuhns, Bremen, IN

Quick Beef Stew

2 cups water
1 quart canned beef chunks
¼ cup ThermFlo
¼ cup flour
½ cup water
4 to 6 potatoes, cooked and cubed
1 pint canned peas
1 pint canned carrots
Salt, pepper, and garlic powder to taste

In saucepan, bring 2 cups water and beef to boil. In bowl, blend ThermFlo, flour, and ½ cup water. Add to beef and stir until thickened. Add potatoes, peas, and carrots. Season with salt, pepper, and garlic powder to suit your taste.

Andrew and Lizzie Miller, Dorset, OH

Chili Soup

2½ pounds ground beef
Onion
Salt and pepper
2 quarts pork and beans
2 quarts tomato juice
1 cup brown sugar
½ cup pickle relish
½ tablespoon chili powder
1 quart water
Cheese, shredded
Sour cream

In kettle, fry beef with onions, salt, and pepper to your taste. Add pork and beans, tomato juice, brown sugar, relish, chili powder, and water. Simmer for 20 to 30 minutes. Serve with cheese and dab of sour cream.

Carolyn Lambright, LaGrange, IN

Hearty Hamburger Soup

2 tablespoons butter
1 pound ground beef
1 cup chopped onion
1 cup diced potatoes
1 cup sliced carrots
½ cup chopped green pepper
2 cups tomato juice
1½ teaspoons salt
¼ teaspoon pepper
1 teaspoon seasoned salt
4 cups milk, divided
¼ cup flour

In saucepan, melt butter and brown beef. Add onion and cook until transparent. Stir in potatoes, carrots, green peppers, tomato juice, salt, pepper, and seasoned salt. Cover and cook on low heat 20 to 25 minutes until vegetables are tender. In bowl, combine 1 cup milk and flour. Stir into soup and bring to boil. Add remaining milk.

This makes a large amount. I often use canned hamburger and carrots.

Mrs. Menno Miller, Gallipolis, OH
Verena Wickey, Monroe, IN

Meatball Garden Stew

1 pound ground beef
4 tablespoons flour, divided
1 teaspoon salt
Dash pepper
1 egg
¼ cup milk
¼ cup chopped onion
1 tablespoon butter
1 onion or garlic clove, minced
1 (14.5 ounce) can beef broth
⅔ cup water
½ teaspoon dried thyme
6 medium potatoes, quartered
6 medium carrots, halved lengthwise
6 green onions, chopped
3 cups fresh, frozen, or canned peas

In bowl, combine ground beef, 2 tablespoons flour, salt, pepper, egg, milk, and onion. Mix well. Form into 1-inch balls. In skillet, melt butter and fry minced onion or garlic for 1 minute. Brown meatballs on all sides. Push meatballs to side. Blend 2 tablespoons flour into drippings. Add broth, water, and thyme. Cook, stirring constantly, until thickened. Add potatoes, carrots, and green onions. Stir into sauce. Cover and simmer 30 to 35 minutes until vegetables are tender. Add peas. Cook 10 minutes more. Yields 6 servings.

Mrs. Menno Miller, Gallipolis, OH

Skillet Casserole

1 pound ground beef
1 small onion
Salt and pepper to taste
Potatoes, shredded
Carrots, shredded
1 cup water
¾ cup milk
1 tablespoon flour
Velveeta cheese

In skillet, brown beef and onion. Salt and pepper to taste. Fill skillet with enough potatoes and carrots for your family. Pour water over all and simmer 20 minutes with lid on. In bowl, whisk together milk and flour. Pour over casserole and simmer a little longer. Top with Velveeta cheese before serving.

Orpha Yoder, Dundee, OH

Meat, Peas, Taters, and Cheese

4 cups mashed potatoes
16 ounces frozen peas, thawed but uncooked
8 thick slices Velveeta cheese
2 pounds ground beef
½ cup chopped onion
1 teaspoon salt
½ teaspoon pepper
2 tablespoons steak sauce
2 teaspoons mustard
1 cup shredded cheese (optional)

In greased 9x13-inch baking pan, spread mashed potatoes. Scatter peas over potatoes and top with sliced cheese. In skillet, brown beef with onions; drain. Add salt, pepper, steak sauce, and mustard. Spoon mixture over cheese. Top with shredded cheese if desired. Cover and bake at 350 degrees for 25 to 30 minutes.

Sara Yoder, Mt. Gilead, OH

BBQ Burgers

2 pounds ground beef
1 egg, beaten
½ cup quick oats
½ teaspoon onion salt
½ teaspoon garlic salt
¼ teaspoon pepper
¼ teaspoon salt
Hamburger buns
Toppings of choice

In bowl, mix ground beef, egg, oats, onion salt, garlic salt, pepper, and salt. Shape into hamburger patties. Grill on each side and baste with barbecue sauce. Serve on buns with toppings of choice.

Mervin and Lorene Miller, Whittemore, MI

Sloppy Joes

1 pound ground beef
½ cup chopped onion
½ cup green pepper
1 tablespoon brown sugar
2 tablespoons mustard
1 teaspoon vinegar
1 cup ketchup
½ teaspoon ground cloves

In skillet, brown beef and crumble. Add onion, pepper, brown sugar, mustard, vinegar, ketchup, and cloves. Let simmer for 20 minutes.

Margaret Wengerd, Bryant, IN

Magic Meatballs

1 pound ground **beef**
2 cups bread cubes
1 package dry onion mix
1 egg, beaten
1 tablespoon parsley flakes
1 cup ketchup
⅓ cup lemon juice
⅓ cup brown sugar

Mix beef, bread, onion mix, egg, and parsley together and shape into balls. Place in baking pan. In bowl, mix ketchup, lemon juice, and brown sugar. Pour over meatballs. Bake at 350 degrees for 45 minutes.

Esther Schwartz, Harrisville, PA

Savory Meatloaf

2 pounds ground **beef**
¼ cup chopped onion
1 cup oatmeal
2½ teaspoons salt
1 egg
¼ teaspoon pepper
1 teaspoon mustard
¼ cup ketchup
1 cup tomato juice

In bowl, mix all ingredients and form into loaf. Bake at 350 degrees for 1 hour. Add glaze when almost done. (This mixture freezes well.)

Glaze:

½ cup brown sugar
1½ teaspoons mustard
1 tablespoon Worcestershire sauce
Vinegar

In bowl, blend brown sugar, mustard, Worcestershire sauce, and enough vinegar to make mixture that is slightly thick. Spread over meatloaf and return to oven for final minutes.

Kristina Mast, New Holstein, WI

Tender T-Bone Steaks

We didn't like steaks until we used this recipe.

6 to 8 steaks
¼ cup plus 1 tablespoon real salt
1 tablespoon baking soda
¼ cup white vinegar

Place steaks in container. Cover with water. In bowl, mix salt, baking soda, and vinegar. Pour over steaks. Refrigerate for 2 days. Drain brine and lightly season with steak seasoning. Let warm to room temperature. Grill at 300 to 350 degrees.

Sue Ellen Borkholder, Sturgis, MI

BBQ Poorman's Steak

1 pound ground beef
1 cup milk
¼ teaspoon pepper
1 teaspoon salt
1 cup cracker crumbs
1 small onion, chopped

In bowl, mix all ingredients together. Press into cookie sheet. Freeze until firm. Cut into squares. Grill or bake meat until almost done through. Cover in sauce and bake at 350 degrees for 1 hour.

Sauce:

6 tablespoons brown sugar
½ cup ketchup
¼ cup water
½ tablespoon vinegar
1 tablespoon liquid smoke
¼ teaspoon mustard

In bowl, mix all ingredients together.

Janet Weaver, Lititz, PA

Melt in Your Mouth Roast

4 to 5 pounds **beef roast**
1 can cream of celery soup
12 ounces cola (i.e. Coke)
Montreal steak seasoning or other seasoning of choice

Place meat in baking dish and pour soup over top and sides. Pour cola over all and sprinkle with seasoning. Cover and bake at 300 degrees for 3 to 3½ hours.

Salomie E. Glick, Howard, PA

Beef Roast

3 to 4 pound beef roast
Brown sugar

Rub roast all over with brown sugar. Place in roasting pan and cover. Bake at 225 degrees overnight or for 6 to 8 hours. Remove juices and thicken for gravy, if desired. Do not salt before roasting as it will dry out meat.

Mary Anna King, Bellefonte, PA

Roast Beef

Rub **beef roast** with oil on both sides. Place in roasting pan and bake, uncovered, at 450 degrees for 45 minutes, flipping halfway through. Remove from oven and turn heat down to 250 degrees. Pour few inches of water into roast pan. Salt liberally and pepper lightly. Slice onion into rings and sprinkle over roast. Bake at 250 degrees for 5 to 6 hours or longer until fork tender. Halfway through baking you can add potatoes and carrots if desired.

Linda Fisher, Ronks, PA

Liver Patties

If your **beef liver** is tough, try grinding it. Season with salt and pepper as desired. Fry like hamburger patties. Chopped onion and beaten eggs may be added to ground liver before making patties. A little flour can be used to coat patties. Ground liver doesn't look very appetizing but finished product is delicious.

Simon and Ida Miller, Clark, MO

Quick Jerky

1 cup sugar
¾ cup seasoning salt
½ cup pepper
5 pounds beef, venison, elk, or other meat cut into thin strips
4 ounces liquid smoke
4 ounces Worcestershire sauce

In shaker, combine sugar, seasoning salt, and pepper. In shallow pan, arrange layer of meat strips. Sprinkle with seasonings. Cover with ¼ to ⅓ of the liquid smoke and Worcestershire sauce. Add another layer of meat and sprinkle with seasonings, liquid smoke, and Worcestershire sauce. Repeat until all meat is in pan and covered. Marinate for 8 hours. Cover oven racks with aluminum foil. Arrange meat strips on foil in single layer. Set oven on lowest temperature setting. Leave oven door ajar and bake 4 to 8 hours or until done to preference.

Mrs. Daniel Schwartz, Geneva, IN

Bologna

40 pounds beef
10 pounds pork
¾ pound Tender Quick
¾ pound salt
3 tablespoons liquid smoke
1 tablespoon curry powder or 1 ounce coriander
3 scant ounces pepper
1 gallon cold water
1 teaspoon mace
1 scant tablespoon garlic powder

Coat chunks of beef and pork in Tender Quick and salt. Grind meat twice. Cover and let meat cure 24 hours. Add liquid smoke, curry powder, pepper, cold water, mace, and garlic powder, mixing well. Pack meat into canning jar and cold pack for 3 hours to seal.

Simon and Ida Miller, Clark, MO

Sandwich Meat

- 7 pounds ground beef, ground twice
- 4 teaspoons sea salt
- 2 teaspoons fennel seed
- 1 teaspoon dry mustard
- 1 teaspoon paprika
- 1 teaspoon garlic salt
- 1 teaspoon sage
- 1 teaspoon pepper
- Sprinkle red pepper
- 2 tablespoons maple syrup
- ½ cup water
- ¼ cup cornstarch

In large bowl, mix all ingredients together well. Fill 7 wide-mouth pint canning jars. Process at 10 pounds pressure for 1 hour. To use, slide out of jar and slice for sandwiches.

Mrs. Rebecca Herschberger, Bear Lake, MI

Pepperoni

3 pounds ground beef, pork, or venison
1 tablespoon fennel seed
1 tablespoon anise seed
2 tablespoons salt
1 teaspoon garlic powder
2 teaspoons paprika
1½ teaspoons ground red pepper

In bowl, mix all ingredients well. Divide into 8 equal portions and form into rolls. Place on cookie sheet and refrigerate, uncovered, overnight. Next morning, bake at 350 degrees for 1 hour, turning once. Let cool. Slice and freeze. A cheese knife works well to slice.

Barbara Stutzman, Apple Creek, OH

Hamburger to Can

20 pounds beef, cut up
6 tablespoons salt
2 tablespoons pepper
½ tablespoon red pepper
1 tablespoon mustard
½ cup organic raw sugar

Spread meat out on table. In bowl, blend salt, pepper, red pepper, mustard, and sugar. Scatter seasoning over meat and mix thoroughly. Run meat through grinder twice. Pack meat into canning jars, leaving head space. Cold pack for 3 hours to cook and seal.

Simon and Ida Miller, Clark, MO

Eggs

Coffee Eggnog

4 eggs, chilled
4 cups cold milk
⅓ cup maple syrup, chilled
1 tablespoon instant coffee
2 teaspoons vanilla

In bowl, use an eggbeater to mix all ingredients. Serves 2 to 4.

Orla and Alice Petersheim, Dalton, WI

Poached Eggs in Tomato Juice

1 quart tomato juice
Salt, pepper, and sugar to taste
2 cups water
Eggs

In large skillet, season tomato juice to taste with salt, pepper, and sugar. Add water. Heat to almost boiling. Juice should be 1½ inches deep in skillet. Gently drop in eggs and simmer, covered, for 3 to 5 minutes. Serve eggs and juice hot over buttered toast.

Mrs. Menno Miller, Gallipolis, OH

Simply Eggs

These eggs are a lot like poached eggs but you avoid the extra chore of washing all the little egg cups.

Butter
3 tablespoons water
Salt and pepper to taste
12 eggs

In large skillet, melt butter. Add water. Crack eggs into pan and sprinkle with salt and pepper. Cover with lid and let set on very low heat for 20 minutes. The nice thing about this method is that you don't need to flip the eggs. They are soft and tasty if cooked until just set. Overcooked eggs are rubbery. When eggs are done, vent lid. (I use a bread tie between pan and lid.)

Wilma Troyer, Kenton, OH

Creamed Eggs

6 eggs, hard boiled and peeled
6 tablespoons butter
6 tablespoons flour
1½ teaspoons salt
Dash of pepper
3 cups milk
4 slices bacon, fried, or
½ cup fried sausage
Toast or biscuits
Shredded cheese (optional)

In heavy saucepan, melt butter. Add flour, salt, and pepper. Stir until well blended. Slowly add milk, stirring constantly. Cook until smooth. Chop eggs and crumble meat into sauce. Serve on toast or biscuits sprinkled with cheese. Yields 6 to 8 servings.

Mrs. Albert L. Yoder, Stanwood, MI

Hidden Eggs

4 tablespoons butter, divided
Bread, cubed
6 to 7 eggs
Salt and pepper to taste
Cheese, shredded

In glass casserole dish, melt 2 tablespoons butter. Put bread in pan to cover bottom. Crack eggs onto bread cubes. Sprinkle with salt and pepper. Cube one or more slices bread to cover eggs. Drizzle 2 tablespoons butter over bread and dot with cheese. Bake at 375 to 400 degrees for 15 to 20 minutes or until eggs are done.

Eli and Laura Petersheim, Kenton, OH

Cheesy Egg Puff

½ cup flour
1 teaspoon baking powder
1 teaspoon salt
10 eggs
4 cups shredded cheese
2 cups cottage cheese
½ cup melted butter

In small bowl, combine flour, baking powder, and salt. In large bowl, lightly beat eggs and add cheese and cottage cheese. Add butter. Stir in dry mixture. Place in 9x13-inch pan. Bake at 350 degrees for 35 to 40 minutes. Serve immediately.

Sharon Miller, Auburn, KY

Ziplock Bag Omelet

Put **egg** in zip closure bag. Seal and squash egg around to mix. Add whatever seasonings you prefer and include fried sausage, bacon bits, chopped hotdog, onion, green pepper, tator tots, cheese, and/or whatever desired. Drop sealed bag into kettle of boiling water and cook 13 minutes.

Eli and Laura Petersheim, Kenton, OH

Cheesy Omelets

3 to 4 eggs
Salt and pepper to taste
Cheese, sliced
Potato, cooked and shredded
Ham, chunked, or any cooked meat of choice

Beat eggs well and put into buttered skillet or omelet pan so that you have a thin layer of egg. Sprinkle with salt and pepper. Flip egg when partially set. Put slices of cheese on top of eggs. On one half of eggs put potatoes and ham. Fold other half of egg over top. Cook until cheese melts. Slide omelet onto platter to serve.

Ida Bontrager, Kenton, OH

Omelet Pie

3 cups frozen shredded hashbrowns
6 eggs
½ teaspoon onion powder
½ teaspoon salt
⅛ teaspoon pepper
⅛ teaspoon thyme
½ cup milk
1 cup shredded Swiss cheese
½ cup diced cooked bacon or ham
½ cup chopped sweet banana pepper
1 to 2 fresh tomatoes

Put hashbrowns in cake pan and bake at 350 degrees for about 15 minutes or until heated through and then crumble. In bowl, beat eggs. Add onion powder, salt, pepper, thyme, and milk. Mix in hashbrowns, cheese, bacon, and peppers. Pour into greased casserole dish. Bake at 350 degrees for 40 to 45 minutes or until center is done. Cut into squares. Garnish with fresh tomato slices just before serving.

Esther L. Miller, Fredericktown, OH

Morning Mix-Up

1 cup cooked shredded potatoes
½ cup cooked diced ham
¼ cup diced onion
1 tablespoon oil
3 eggs
Salt and pepper to taste
½ cup shredded cheddar cheese

In skillet, sauté potatoes, ham, and onions in oil until potatoes are tender. In bowl, beat eggs and season with salt and pepper. Pour over potatoes. Cook, stirring occasionally, until eggs are set. Remove from heat and gently stir in cheese.

Maria Zook, Dalton, OH

Breakfast Casserole

Prepare this the night before serving. It's nice for company on a Sunday morning.

20 to 24 eggs
1 cup milk
Salt and pepper to taste
1 cup cooked meat of choice (bacon, sausage, ham)
1 cup cooked and shredded potatoes
1 to 2 cups shredded cheese

In bowl, beat eggs. Beat in milk and season to taste with salt and pepper. Pour into greased 9x13-inch pan. Sprinkle in meat and potatoes. Top with cheese. Refrigerate overnight. Bake at 350 to 375 degrees for 45 to 60 minutes.

Grace Zimmerman, Shiloh, OH

Country Style Scrambled Eggs

½ cup chopped onion
½ cup chopped green pepper
2 cups cubed or chopped potatoes
3 tablespoons butter
6 eggs, beaten
2 tablespoons milk
Salt to taste
¼ teaspoon pepper
1 cup diced ham
1 cup shredded white cheddar cheese

In skillet, fry onion, pepper, and potatoes in butter. When vegetables are soft, beat eggs with milk, salt, and pepper. Add to vegetables and stir to cook. Add ham and cheese and mix until melted. Serve immediately.

Lizzie N. Christner, Berne IN

Sausage, Zucchini, Egg Scramble

1 pound ground sausage
1 medium zucchini, cubed but not peeled
6 eggs
Salt and pepper to taste
Cheese shredded

In skillet, fry sausage. When almost done, add zucchini. When zucchini is soft, add eggs, salt, and pepper. Stir frequently. When eggs are set, top with cheese.

Erma Shetler, Millersburg, OH

Mustard Eggs

1 cup vinegar
½ cup water
1 cup sugar
2 tablespoons dry mustard
1 tablespoon garlic powder
1 tablespoon onion powder
2 teaspoons salt
1½ teaspoons yellow food coloring
10 hard-boiled eggs

In bowl, mix vinegar, water, sugar, mustard, garlic powder, onion powder, salt, and food coloring. Add eggs, cover, and refrigerate 3 days before serving.

Susie King, Allenwood, PA

Pickled Eggs

18 eggs
1 cup beet juice, drained from 1 pint pickled beets
1 cup sugar
1 cup white vinegar
1 teaspoon salt

In large pot, carefully place eggs and cover with water. Bring to hard boil. Remove from heat, cover, and let stand 12 minutes. Remove from pot and place in bowl of ice water. Peel chilled eggs and place in half-gallon jar.

If you don't have a full cup of beet juice after draining your pickled beets, add water to drained beets and shake jar to get a bit more juice.

In small saucepan, mix together beet juice, sugar, vinegar, and salt. Bring to boil. Pour hot syrup over eggs and refrigerate. Shake the jar a few times a day so eggs are evenly pickled. After 3 days, eggs should be ready to eat. They should keep for a month.

Saloma Zook, Fredericksburg, OH

Homemade Mayonnaise

2 eggs
1½ teaspoon salt
1 teaspoon ground mustard
½ teaspoon paprika
2 tablespoons lemon juice
2 tablespoons vinegar
2 cups oil, divided

In blender, combine eggs, salt, mustard, and paprika. Blend then scrape down sides of blender. Add lemon juice. Very slowly run blender and drizzle in ½ cup oil and vinegar. Blend and drizzle in remaining oil until mayonnaise reaches desired consistency.

Barbie Beiler, Gap, PA

Battered Fish

1 egg white
3 teaspoons baking powder
1 teaspoon oil
1 teaspoon salt
1 cup flour
¾ cup water
3½ pounds fish

In bowl, beat egg whites until stiff. In another bowl, mix baking powder, oil, salt, flour, and water. Stir in egg whites. Dip fish pieces into batter and deep fry.

Verena Wickey, Monroe, IN

Ham and Potato Soup

1½ quarts cubed potatoes
½ cup butter
½ cup flour
1½ quarts milk
2 teaspoons salt
½ teaspoon pepper
1 teaspoon garlic salt
¼ cup chopped onions
1½ pounds ham, cubed
Few slices Velveeta cheese

In saucepan, place potatoes and cover with water. Cook until softened. In skillet, brown butter and flour. Slowly add milk, salt, pepper, garlic salt, and onions. Add mixture to cooked potatoes in cooking water. Stir in ham and cheese, stirring until cheese melts.

Kristina Mast, New Holstein, WI
Lena Miller, Gallipolis, OH

Meat and Vegetable Dinner

2 to 3 tablespoons lard or butter
2 tablespoons flour
4 pork chops or meat of choice
Carrots, sliced
Potatoes, sliced
Onions, sliced
Seasoned salt
Salt
Pepper
½ to ¾ cup water
Cheese, shredded

In 9- to 10-inch stainless steel skillet, melt lard then sprinkle with flour. Tenderize pork chops with meat hammer or knife. Lay single layer of pork chops in skillet. Fry one side for 10 to 15 minutes. Turn pork chops. Layer in carrots, potatoes, and onions on top of pork chops. Sprinkle with seasoned salt, salt, and pepper to taste. Pour water over all and cover with tight lid. Let cook over low heat for 40 to 60 minutes until vegetables are tender. Don't cook too fast or high as it can burn. When done, top with shredded cheese if desired.

Jerry and Ida Petersheim, Kenton, OH

Stuffed Pork Loin

A family favorite at our Christmas dinner.

Pork tenderloin
1 large head cabbage
1½ pounds onions
1 pound kale
1 tablespoon crushed red pepper
1 tablespoon ground red pepper
1 tablespoon ground black pepper
1 tablespoon mustard seed
1 tablespoon celery seed
1 tablespoon salt

Remove outer leaves from cabbage and set aside. Chop cabbage head, onions, and kale finely. Mix vegetables in bowl and add red peppers, black pepper, mustard seed, celery seed, and salt. Place tenderloin in roasting pan that has lid. Cut 2 slits lengthwise down tenderloin to within 1 inch of bottom. Fill slits with mixture. Pack tightly. Place remaining mixture over top. Cover all with cabbage leaves and place on lid. Bake at 275 degrees for 2 hours or until internal thermometer of meat reads 145 to 150 degrees.

Note: This can be baked a few days ahead of your dinner and served cold.

Chris and Magdalena Swarey, Charlotte Hall, MD

Pulled Pork

1 teaspoon salt
1 teaspoon paprika
1 teaspoon chili powder
½ teaspoon garlic powder
⅛ teaspoon red pepper
4 pounds **pork shoulder**, cut into 3 pieces
1 onion, thinly sliced
½ teaspoon hot pepper sauce
½ cup brown sugar
½ cup ketchup
⅓ cup vinegar
¼ cup tomato paste
¼ cup water
2 tablespoons mustard
2 tablespoons Worcestershire sauce

In bowl, mix salt, paprika, chili powder, garlic powder, and red pepper. Rub over pork. In 6-quart or larger slow cooker, combine pork, onion, hot pepper sauce, brown sugar, ketchup, vinegar, tomato paste, water, mustard, and Worcestershire sauce. Cover and cook on low for 6 to 8 hours. Remove pork and cool 10 minutes. Shred pork using forks. Combine with sauce from slow cooker. Serve on rolls, adding barbecue sauce if desired.

Menno and Esther Yoder, Berlin, PA

Canned Fresh Ham in Brine

- Fresh uncured, unsalted **ham**, cubed
- 2 cups Tender Quick
- 2 tablespoons hickory smoke
- 2 cups brown sugar
- 1 gallon water

Pack ham loosely in canning jars. In bowl, mix Tender Quick, hickory smoke, brown sugar, and water. Fill jars with brine. Cold pack for 1 hour to seal.

Mrs. Rebecca Herschberger, Bear Lake, MI

Brine for Smoked Whole Ham

- 1 pound salt
- 1 pound plus 4 ounces brown sugar
- 1 ounce pepper
- 1 pound Tender Quick
- 1 whole raw **ham**

Combine salt, brown sugar, pepper, and Tender Quick. Coat whole raw ham and cover with water. Soak for 3 to 5 days. Remove from brine and smoke.

Marilyn Schwartz, Monroe, IN

Sausage

- 25 pounds ground **pork**
- 1½ pounds ice water
- 7 ounces canning salt
- 2 ounces pepper
- ¼ ounce nutmeg
- ¼ ounce ground ginger
- 1 cup brown sugar (optional)
- ¼ ounce red pepper (optional)

Mix all together well. Freeze or can as desired.

Kathryn Hochstetler, Spartansburg, PA

Poultry

Chicken Salad

A quick way to make a tasty lunch with leftover chicken.

½ cup mayonnaise
1 tablespoon honey
2 teaspoons white vinegar
1 teaspoon Dijon mustard
½ teaspoon seasoned salt
½ teaspoon pepper
2 cups chopped, cooked **chicken**
⅓ cup chopped sweet dill pickles
4 hard-boiled eggs
1 stalk celery, chopped
2 tablespoons diced onion

In medium bowl, mix mayonnaise, honey, vinegar, and mustard. Add seasoned salt and pepper. Fold in chicken, pickles, eggs, celery, and onion. Refrigerate for at least 30 minutes before serving. Serve on bread, crackers, or lettuce leaves.

Saloma Zook, Fredericksburg, OH

White Chili

1 pound **chicken** breast, cubed
1 onion, chopped
1½ teaspoons garlic powder
1 tablespoon oil
2 (16 ounce) cans great northern beans
1 pint chicken broth
¼ teaspoon red pepper (optional)
½ teaspoon pepper
1 teaspoon salt
1 teaspoon cumin
1 teaspoon oregano
1 cup milk
1 cup sour cream

In kettle, fry chicken and onion with garlic powder in oil for 5 minutes. Add beans, broth, red pepper, pepper, salt, cumin, and oregano. Simmer at least 15 minutes. Just before serving, add milk and sour cream.

Elsie Beiler, Fredericksburg, OH

Chicken Noodle Soup

4 quarts **chicken**, cooked and cubed
1 gallon cooked noodles
4 quarts chicken broth
½ gallon cubed carrots
½ gallon cubed potatoes
2 quarts diced celery
1 quart canned lima beans
½ cup chicken base
Celery salt to taste
Salt to taste

In large pot, mix chicken, noodles, and broth. In saucepan, cook carrots, potatoes, celery, lima beans, chicken base, celery salt, and salt until nearly soft. Mix into chicken and noodles. Bring to boiling point. Divide into prepared quart jars. Cold pack for 2 hours. Yields approximately 20 quarts.

Mrs. Albert L. Yoder, Stanwood, MI

Chicken Burgers

When we have old hens to butcher, we remove meat from the bone and grind it.

- 1 pound ground chicken
- 1 egg
- 5 crackers, crushed
- Salt and pepper to taste
- Chicken breading or flour
- Butter

Mix chicken, egg, and crackers. Season to taste with salt and pepper. Form patties and roll in breading. Fry in butter.

Mrs. Levi (Elsie) Schlabach, Big Prairie, OH

Deep-Fried Chicken Nuggets

- 1 chicken breast, cut into bite-sized pieces
- 1 egg, beaten
- ½ cup water
- 1 teaspoon salt
- ¼ cup cornmeal
- ¼ cup flour
- ¼ cup wheat flour
- 1 quart coconut oil

In bowl, mix egg, water, salt, cornmeal, flour, and wheat flour. Heat oil until it reaches 375 degrees. Dip chicken into batter and drop into hot oil one at a time. Fry for 3 to 5 minutes. Yummy served with barbecue sauce. We also use this batter for larger pieces of fish and onion rings.

Daniel and Mary Shetler, Homer, MI

Chicken Fingers

- 1 tablespoon flour
- 1 teaspoon poultry seasoning
- ¾ teaspoon garlic salt
- ½ teaspoon paprika
- ¼ teaspoon pepper
- ⅛ to ¼ teaspoon cayenne pepper (optional)
- 1½ pounds boneless, skinless **chicken** breasts cut into ½-inch strips
- 2 tablespoons butter

In large bowl, combine flour, poultry seasoning, garlic salt, paprika, pepper, and cayenne pepper. Add chicken and toss or shake to coat. In skillet, cook chicken in butter for 8 to 10 minutes or until juices run clear.

Susie King, Allenwood, PA

Honey BBQ Boneless Wings

5 pounds boneless chicken breast
2 cups milk
2 eggs
6 cups flour
3 tablespoons salt
1½ teaspoons pepper
1 tablespoon paprika
2 teaspoons garlic powder
2 teaspoons cayenne pepper (optional)
Cooking oil
Sauce (recipe below)

Cut chicken into small pieces. In bowl, whisk together milk and eggs. In another bowl, mix flour, salt, pepper, paprika, garlic powder, and cayenne pepper. Dip chicken in egg mixture then roll in dry mixture. Repeat egg dip and roll in dry mixture again. Deep fry at 375 degrees for 5 to 7 minutes. Lay on rack or paper towel to dry a little. Then layer in roaster pan. Lay down one layer of chicken and coat with some sauce. Repeat chicken then sauce layers until all chicken is in pan and coated. We also like the chicken without sauce.

Sauce:

4 cups brown sugar
1 cup water
⅓ cup Worcestershire sauce
⅓ cup barbecue sauce
¼ teaspoon pepper
¾ teaspoon mustard
¾ tablespoon onion salt
¾ tablespoon salt
2 pints ketchup

In saucepan, mix together all ingredients and heat but don't boil.

Regina Miller, Nappanee, IN

Chicken Veggie Bake

An easy and very adaptable recipe.

1 whole broiler chicken
4 large potatoes
4 medium carrots
Salt and other seasonings to taste

Cut chicken into pieces. Cut potatoes and carrots into sticks, like for French fries. Put all in large roaster and add little water to the bottom. Season with salt and other favorite seasonings to your taste. Cover and bake at 350 degrees for 1½ to 2 hours until chicken is done and tender.

Mary Miller, Junction City, OH

Chicken Pie

2 cups sliced carrots
4 cups chopped potatoes
4 cups peas
1 cup chopped celery
⅓ cup chopped onion
5 cups chicken broth
1 cup water
1 tablespoon chicken base
1 teaspoon poultry seasoning
1 stick butter
4 teaspoons salt
Pepper to taste
Red pepper to taste
1⅓ cups flour
1½ cups water
6 cups cooked and chopped chicken (about 5 pounds raw)
6 (9 inch) unbaked pie shells with tops

Prepare carrots, potatoes, peas, celery, and onion by parboiling, separately if necessary to cook but not too soft or mushy. In kettle, heat chicken broth, 1 cup water, and chicken base. Add poultry seasoning, butter, salt, pepper, and red pepper; bring to boil. In bowl, blend flour and 1½ cups water to form paste. Add to boiling broth to thicken. Mix in chicken and cooked and drained vegetables. Ladle into 6 pie shells. Top each with crust. Bake at 350 degrees for 1 hour.

Linda Fisher, Ronks, PA

Chicken Stir-Fry

Butter
Olive oil
1 large onion, cut coarsely
Potatoes, chopped
Carrots, diced
Bell peppers, chopped
Green beans, fresh cut
3 eggs, fried and chopped
1 cup uncooked rice, cook as directed
1 pound chicken breast, cooked and diced
Salt and pepper to taste
Paprika to taste
Ranch or sweet and sour dressing

In a skillet, coat bottom with butter and oil. Fry onion, potatoes, carrots, peppers, and beans until tender. Add eggs, cooked rice, and chicken. Season with salt, pepper, and paprika to taste. Serve with ranch or sweet and sour dressing.

Becky Zook, Navarre, OH

Oven Chicken

1 cup cracker crumbs
¼ cup flour
1 tablespoon powdered sugar
1 teaspoon Accent
½ teaspoon salt
¼ teaspoon seasoned salt
¼ teaspoon paprika
¼ teaspoon garlic salt
8 pieces chicken
½ cup butter, melted

In bowl, mix cracker crumbs, flour, powdered sugar, Accent, salt, seasoned salt, paprika, and garlic salt. Dip chicken in butter then into crumb mixture. Place on greased baking pan. Bake at 350 degrees for 1 hour.

Kristina Miller, Decatur, IN

Herb Roasted Chicken and Potatoes

8 chicken thighs
1 onion, chopped
1 sweet potato, chopped
3 red potatoes, chopped
¼ cup butter
½ teaspoon garlic powder
½ teaspoon salt
½ teaspoon pepper
1 teaspoon brown sugar
½ teaspoon chicken seasoning
¼ teaspoon red pepper
1 tablespoon parsley flakes
6 strips bacon, cut into large pieces

Place chicken, onion, sweet potato, and red potatoes in greased 9x13-inch pan. In saucepan, melt butter and add garlic powder, salt, pepper, brown sugar, chicken seasoning, red pepper, and parsley. Pour sauce over all, making sure everything is evenly coated. Place bacon pieces on top. Bake at 350 degrees for 1½ hours.

Titus Yoder, Salisbury, PA

Tender Crusty Chicken

1 cup flour
½ cup cornmeal
1 teaspoon salt
3½ teaspoons seasoned salt
1 teaspoon paprika
¼ teaspoon cream of tartar
Egg
Milk
4 to 5 pounds chicken on the bone
Oil

In bowl, combine flour, cornmeal, salt, seasoned salt, paprika, and cream of tartar. In another bowl, beat together egg and enough milk to cover chicken. Dip egg-washed chicken in dry mixture to coat and deep fry in hot oil. As chicken is done, place in roaster in oven to stay warm, but don't cover the pan or close oven door.

Lucinda Schwartz, Monroe, IN

Cheesy Chicken Breast

8 boneless, skinless **chicken** breast
8 slices Velveeta cheese
2 cans cream of chicken soup
½ cup water
⅔ cup melted butter
2 cups crushed Ritz crackers

Cut chicken in half and place in 9x13-inch baking pan. Put cheese on top of chicken. In bowl, mix soup and water. Pour over chicken. In another bowl, combine butter and crackers. Spread on top of chicken. Bake uncovered at 350 degrees for 45 to 60 minutes.

Lorina Miller, Mechanicstown, OH

Delicious Chicken Breast

1½ pounds **chicken** breast
1 package Italian dressing mix
⅓ cup brown sugar
½ tablespoon garlic powder
Salt and pepper to taste

Combine chicken breast, dressing mix, brown sugar, garlic powder, salt, and pepper and refrigerate for 24 hours. Put chicken in baking dish and bake uncovered at 375 degrees for 25 to 30 minutes.

Barbara Miller, Big Prairie, OH
Mrs. Atlee (Clara) Yoder, Big Prairie, OH

Barbecue Chicken

Sprinkle salt on **chicken** pieces. Roll chicken in flour or half flour/half cornmeal. Place in baking pan and bake at 400 degrees for 15 minutes. Reduce heat to 350 degrees and bake 45 minutes. Spoon barbecue sauce over chicken once or twice while baking 10 to 15 minutes longer or until meat is tender.

Moses and Leah Renno, Jackson, OH

Marinated Grilled Chicken

3 pounds **chicken** tenders or breast, sliced to 1 inch thick
1 cup mayonnaise
1 teaspoon celery salt
1 teaspoon seasoned salt
1 teaspoon onion salt
½ teaspoon garlic salt
¾ teaspoon pepper
¾ teaspoon paprika
1 teaspoon curry powder

Place chicken in container. In a bowl, mix mayonnaise, celery salt, seasoned salt, onion salt, garlic salt, pepper, paprika, and curry powder. Coat chicken well. Marinate for 1 to 3 days in refrigerator. Grill at 450 degrees for 5 to 10 minutes on each side or until done. Delicious and tender.

Grace Zimmerman, Shiloh, OH

Sweet and Sour Chicken

2 pounds **chicken** breast, cut into 1-inch chunks
Salt and pepper to taste
2 cups cornstarch
2 eggs, beaten
¼ cup oil
¾ cup sugar
½ cup vinegar
¼ cup ketchup
½ teaspoon garlic powder
1 tablespoon soy sauce
Brown rice, prepared

In bowl, season chicken with salt and pepper to taste and toss with cornstarch. Dip in eggs and fry in oil for 2 minutes or until golden. Put into 9x13-inch pan. In bowl, mix sugar, vinegar, ketchup, garlic powder, and soy sauce. Pour over chicken. Bake at 350 degrees for 30 minutes, stirring after 15 minutes, until hot and bubbly. Serve with brown rice.

Carolyn Lambright, LaGrange, IN

Chicken Bologna

35 pounds **chicken**, ground twice
10 pounds bacon, ground (optional)
1½ cups Tender Quick
1 heaping tablespoon pepper
3 tablespoons liquid smoke
1 tablespoon garlic salt or powder

Mix all ingredients and let stand 1 or 2 days in cold place. Put into summer sausage bags and smoke to cure.

Mrs. Enos Wickey, Monroe, IN

How to Tenderize a Tough Old Bird

Chicken pieces
1 cup salt
⅓ to ½ cup vinegar
1 rounded tablespoon baking soda
2 gallons water

Place chicken in large container with lid. Add salt, vinegar, baking soda, and water to cover. Refrigerate for 1 week. Rinse before cooking. You may not need to add salt while cooking. This also works to take the wild taste out of venison.

Sadie Bender, Meyersdale, PA

Turkey Brine

2¼ gallons water
1½ cups salt
¾ cup apple cider vinegar
6 tablespoons baking soda
1½ tablespoons pepper
1 tablespoon ground mustard
1 tablespoon paprika
1 teaspoon garlic powder
2 tablespoons liquid smoke (optional)

Mix all ingredients together. Soak whole turkey in brine for 3 to 5 days. Smoke or cook turkey as desired. This brine can also work well for steak before grilling.

Grace Zimmerman, Shiloh, OH

Chicken Broth

A delicious broth to add to soup or sip when your are sick.

2 to 3 pounds boney **chicken** parts
4 quarts cold water
1 large onion, chopped
Garlic, thyme, sage, and pepper to taste
2 tablespoons vinegar
2 carrots, chopped
1 handful fresh parsley, minced

In large kettle, combine chicken parts, cold water, onion, seasonings, vinegar, and carrots. Let stand 30 to 60 minutes. Turn on heat and bring to boil. Skim foam that comes to top. Reduce heat, cover, and simmer 6 to 24 hours. About 10 minutes before done, stir in parsley. Ladle into quart canning jars and seal in water bath for 10 minutes.

Joann Miller, Fredericktown, OH

Cream of Chicken Soup

1 pound butter
1 cup flour
4 teaspoons salt
2 to 4 cups chopped **chicken**
13 cups **chicken broth**
3 cups milk
Onion, diced (optional)
Celery, diced (optional)
Chicken seasoning (optional)

In stockpot, melt butter. Blend in flour and salt, stirring until smooth and bubbly. Remove from heat. Stir in broth 2 cups at a time. Add milk. Return to heat, stirring constantly until thickened. Add chicken. If desired, season to taste with onion, celery, and/or chicken seasoning. Ladle into half pint jars. Pressure can at 10 pounds pressure for 45 minutes. Yields 20 (½ pint) jars.

Mrs. Ezra (Darla) Yoder, Homer, MI

Vegetables and Herbs

Better is a dinner of herbs where love is,
Than a fatted calf with hatred.

- Proverbs 15:17 NKJV

Vegetables and Herbs Recipes:

Many people will grow a few backyard vegetables and herbs for their own use. Other people with more space will happily grow extra to share, trade, preserve, or sell. It can be fun to find someone with extra green beans to trade for your extra tomatoes. For a fall adventure, find a farm where you can pick out your own pumpkins and play in a corn maze.

RHUBARB

SQUASH

TOMATOES

GARLIC HERB SEASONING

There is nothing better than fresh dried herbs from the garden for this.

- 1 cup **garlic salt**
- 2 tablespoons plus 2 teaspoons **oregano**
- 4 teaspoons **basil**
- 4 teaspoons **marjoram**
- 4 teaspoons **savory** (optional)
- 4 teaspoons **thyme**
- 4 teaspoons **rosemary**

Mix all together and store in airtight container. Great to use on garlic bread or in many warm dishes.

ORLA AND ALICE PETERSHEIM, Dalton, WI

Mint Tea Concentrate

12 quarts water
1½ gallons mint tea leaves, packed
8 to 12 cups sugar

In large kettle, gently boil tea leaves in water for 5 minutes. Remove from heat, cover, and let stand 15 minutes. Remove tea leaves and sweeten to taste. Freeze or can concentrate. Mix 2 parts water to 1 part tea concentrate. It is a mild but refreshing drink.

Tip: Freeze leftover tea in ice cube trays and add tea cubes to your next glass of tea.

Malinda Gingerich, Hartford, KS

Super Tonic

Immune booster and great for sore throats.

Onions
Garlic
Horseradish
Habanero peppers
Jalapeño peppers
Raw apple cider vinegar

Finely chop and grind equal amounts onions, garlic, horseradish, and peppers. Feel free to adjust amount of peppers if too hot. Fill quart jar with the mixture. Fill jar to brim with vinegar. Put on tight lid and shake every day for 2 to 4 weeks. Strain through cheesecloth into bottles. Dispose of solids. Keeps 3 to 4 years if sealed in dark bottles.

Marilyn Schwartz, Monroe, IN

Asparagus

Baked Asparagus

Asparagus
Butter
3 cups milk
4 eggs
Salt and pepper to taste
Sliced hot dogs, cubed ham, or fried and crumbled bacon
1½ cups crushed buttery crackers, divided

In saucepan, steam asparagus in butter. In bowl, mix milk, eggs, salt, and pepper. Add asparagus, hot dogs, and 1 cup crackers. Place in greased casserole dish. Top with ½ cup crackers. Bake at 225 degrees for 1 hour or until knife inserted in center comes out clean.

Bethany Martin, Homer City, PA

Asparagus Casserole

4 cups broken fresh asparagus
½ teaspoon salt
¼ cup butter
2 cups milk
1 teaspoon sour cream and onion powder
⅛ teaspoon pepper
¼ cup flour
4 slices bread, cubed and drizzled with ¼ cup butter

In saucepan, cook asparagus in water with salt. Place cooked asparagus in buttered cake pan. In saucepan, cook together butter, milk, sour cream and onion powder, pepper, and flour until thickened. Pour over asparagus. Top with buttered bread cubes. Bake at 350 degrees for 20 minutes.

Mrs. Joseph Beiler, Woodward, PA

Pickled Asparagus

Asparagus
Garlic, minced
Mustard seed
Red pepper
¾ cup salt
8 cups water
4 cups vinegar

Clean and stack asparagus spears into quart canning jars. To each quart jar add minced garlic, mustard seed, and sprinkle of red pepper. In saucepan, combine salt, water, and vinegar; bring to full boil. Pour hot brine over asparagus to fill jars. Seal jars immediately in hot water bath for 5 minutes.

KATIE ESH, Charlotte Court House, VA

Beans

Honey Green Beans

2 tablespoons bacon grease or butter
¼ onion, sliced
4 cups fresh uncut **green beans**
2 tablespoons honey
1 teaspoon salt

In large skillet, melt bacon grease and add onions, sautéing until onions are translucent. Add green beans. Drizzle with honey and sprinkle with salt. Cover and cook 10 minutes or until slightly crunchy. Uncover and simmer on high for few minutes to reduce juices.

Saloma Zook, Fredericksburg, OH

Coated Green Beans

2 quarts **green beans,** trimmed
½ cup bacon bits
¾ cup browned butter
2 teaspoons Greek seasoning

In kettle, cook beans covered in water until just tender. Drain. Add bacon bits, browned butter, and Greek seasoning. Spread in baking dish. Bake at 400 degrees for 10 to 15 minutes. Don't stir.

Martha Beachy, Butler, OH

Dilly Beans

Green beans, trimmed
½ teaspoon dill seed or 1 dill head
3 garlic cloves
5 cups vinegar
5 cups water
½ cup salt
½ teaspoon cayenne pepper (optional)

Pack quart canning jars tightly with uncut green beans. Add ½ teaspoon dill seed or 1 dill head and 3 garlic cloves (cut in half) to each quart jar. In saucepan, combine vinegar, water, salt, and cayenne pepper and bring to boil. Pour over beans in jars. Seal in hot water bath for 15 minutes.

Anna M. Weaver, Mertztown, PA

Chow Chow

1 quart dry soup beans
1 quart dry lima beans
3 quarts peppers
3 quarts celery
3 quarts watermelon rind
3 quarts green beans
3 quarts pickles
3 quarts carrots
3 quarts cauliflower
1 quart onion
1 quart kidney beans
1 teaspoon turmeric
1 teaspoon celery seed
2 cups sugar
1 cup water
1 cup vinegar

In saucepan, soak dry soup beans and lima beans overnight then cook until just soft. Do not overcook. Scald peppers in boiling water to keep crisp. In individual stockpots, cook celery, watermelon rind, green beans, pickles, carrots, cauliflower, and onion in salted water until just tender (about 20 minutes). Drain well. Mix cooked vegetables with cooked beans, kidney beans, and peppers. Add turmeric and celery seed. In saucepan, combine sugar, water, and vinegar and heat until sugar dissolves. Pour over vegetable mixture. Make more syrup if needed to cover all vegetables. Pack into jars and cold pack 10 minutes.

Sara Yoder, Mt. Gilead, OH

Green Beans to Can

Fill quart jar with cut **green beans**. Add 2 tablespoons vinegar, 1 tablespoon sugar, and 1 teaspoon salt to jar and fill with water. Cold pack for 25 to 30 minutes to seal. When ready to use, rinse beans with cold water before putting in kettle to heat. These are very good to fry with bacon. Add cheese and let melt before serving.

Lori Miller, Middlefield, OH

Lorene Schwartz, Monroe, IN

Barbecued Green Beans

1 quart canned green beans, drained
1 small onion, chopped
6 slices uncooked bacon, cut in pieces
1 cup ketchup
¾ scant cup brown sugar

Mix all ingredients together and bake in covered casserole dish at 350 degrees for 1 hour.

Note: Fresh or frozen green beans can be used but they must be cooked 5 to 10 minutes to tenderize.

Kristina Mast, New Holstein, WI

Overnight Red Beets

Wash **beets** then put in kettle and boil for 10 minutes. Leave lid on and let set overnight. The next morning, peel beets and refrigerate. I like to make enough beets to last several days. To prepare: Put a little butter in pan and slice beets into butter. Add salt to taste. Heat, stirring frequently. I really dislike cold, pickled beets, but these are delicious.

Erma Shetler, Millersburg, OH

Broccoli

Broccoli Cheese Soup

This is our favorite soup.

1 head **broccoli**
3 cups milk
¼ cup flour
½ cup milk
Salt to taste
1 teaspoon chicken base
Velveeta cheese

Cut broccoli and place in saucepan. Add a little water and boil until soft. Add 3 cups milk and heat until almost boiling. In bowl, make paste with flour and ½ cup milk. Stir into soup and bring to boil. Turn off heat and add salt, chicken base, and cheese.

Mrs. Levi (Elsie) Schlabach, Big Prairie, OH

Perfect Broccoli

½ cup water
1 teaspoon sugar
4 cups fresh or frozen chopped **broccoli**
Salt to taste

In saucepan, combine water and sugar. Bring to boil. Add broccoli. Cover and cook 5 to 8 minutes or until just tender. Sprinkle with salt and serve immediately.

Saloma Zook, Fredericksburg, OH

Cabbage

Day-Before Cabbage Salad

We had this salad for my sister's wedding. It is really good with deep-fried fish and noodles.

2 cups salad dressing (like Miracle Whip) or mayonnaise
1½ cups sour cream
1 cup sugar
2 teaspoons salt
8 cups shredded **cabbage**
1 cup fried and crumbled bacon
½ cup peas
4 cups shredded cheddar cheese
2 cups crushed nacho chips
Cherry tomatoes (optional)

In bowl, blend salad dressing, sour cream, sugar, and salt. In extra large bowl, layer cabbage, blended sauce from mixer, bacon, peas, and cheese. Cover and let set overnight. Before serving, toss salad and top with chips and tomatoes.

Kristina Mast, New Holstein, WI

Anna Swartzentruber, West Salem, OH

Creamy Coleslaw

1 small head **cabbage**, shredded
Carrots, shredded
1¼ cups mayonnaise or Miracle Whip salad dressing
½ cup sugar
2 tablespoons vinegar
Celery seed (optional)
¼ teaspoon salt

Combine cabbage and carrots in bowl. In another bowl, blend mayonnaise, sugar, vinegar, celery seed to taste, and salt. Pour over cabbage and mix.

Mrs. Joseph Miller, Navarre, OH

Curtido (Salvadoran Slaw)

1 medium head **cabbage**, shredded
1 cup shredded carrots
1 medium onion, chopped
¼ teaspoon red pepper flakes (optional)
2 tablespoons salt
2 tablespoons minced garlic

Mix all ingredients together in bowl. Let stand 5 to 10 minutes until juicy. Pack mixture into sterile canning jars and cover loosely. Let stand at room temperature for 2 to 3 days. Tighten lids on jars and store in cellar, burping occasionally. Let ferment for at least 2 to 3 weeks before eating.

Ada L. Zook, Hillsboro, OH

Big batch ingredients:

4 large heads **cabbage**, shredded
4 cups shredded carrots
8 medium onions, chopped
4 tablespoons oregano
1 to 2 teaspoons red pepper flakes or 1 cayenne pepper
8 tablespoons salt

Barbara Stutzman, Apple Creek, OH

Simple Sauerkraut

Shred **cabbage** with Salad Master. Add 1 tablespoon sea salt per quart. This is guesswork as cabbage shrinks together when pressed. You want 1 tablespoon salt per finished quart of sauerkraut. Mix cabbage and salt and let set for 10 minutes or until juices form. Pack cabbage into jars, pressing it in to bring liquid to top of cabbage, leaving 1 inch air space. Close jars very tightly. Keep jars at room temperature for 3 days then move to cool canning shelves. That's all! In a few weeks, you can start eating the sauerkraut. When you open jar, keep it in refrigerator. Sometimes I add garlic cloves and onion, chopped, to make it even better.

Gertie Anne Mast, Greenville, PA

Cabbage Casserole

1 medium cabbage, cut into thin wedges
½ cup water
¼ cup butter or margarine
¼ cup flour
2 cups milk
½ teaspoon salt
¼ teaspoon pepper
¾ cup shredded cheddar cheese
½ cup mayonnaise
½ cup finely chopped onion
½ cup finely chopped green pepper
3 tablespoons chili sauce (optional)

In saucepan, cover cabbage with water and cook about 15 minutes. Drain well and place cabbage in casserole dish. Melt butter in saucepan and add flour, stirring until smooth. Gradually add milk, stirring constantly until thick and bubbly. Stir in salt and pepper. Pour over cabbage. Bake at 375 for 20 minutes. In bowl, mix cheese, mayonnaise, onion, green pepper, and chili sauce. Spread over casserole. Bake at 400 degrees for 20 minutes.

Moses and Leah Renno, Jackson, OH

Cabbage with Noodles and Bacon

1 pound bacon
2 to 3 pounds cabbage
1 to 1½ pounds homemade noodles
Salt and pepper to taste

In large skillet, cut bacon into small pieces and fry until crispy. Drain and set bacon aside. Cut cabbage into small slices and fry in bacon grease until tender and slightly browned. In kettle, boil noodles until tender; drain. Combine bacon, cabbage, and noodles and season with salt and pepper before serving. Simple but very delicious.

Clarice Swanchara, Gladwin, MI

Carrots

Seasoned Carrot Fries

7 large carrots
¼ teaspoon pepper
¼ teaspoon smoked paprika
¼ teaspoon salt
1 tablespoon cornstarch
2 tablespoons cooking oil

Wash carrots and cut into fry-like strips. In bowl, mix pepper, paprika, salt, cornstarch, and oil. Pour over carrots and mix to coat well. Grease baking sheet and spread carrots on it evenly. Bake at 375 degrees for 35 minutes or until soft. Serve with dip.

Dip:

6 ounces cream cheese
2 tablespoons butter
1 tablespoon honey
1 tablespoon maple syrup
¾ teaspoon cinnamon

In bowl, mix all ingredients and beat until smoothly combined.

Mary Yoder, Mount Gilead, OH

Scalloped Carrots

12 carrots, sliced
4 tablespoons butter
4 tablespoons flour
2 cups milk
2 cups chopped onion
¼ teaspoon salt
¼ teaspoon celery salt
⅛ teaspoon pepper
1 teaspoon mustard
½ cup diced Velveeta cheese

In saucepan, cook carrots in little water until tender but not too soft. In another saucepan, melt butter, stir in flour and cook until bubbly. Add milk, stirring until it starts to thicken. Add onion, salt, celery salt, pepper, mustard, and cheese.

Rachel Lantz, Strasburg, PA

Good Carrot Cake

2¼ cups whole wheat flour
1½ cups oatmeal
2 teaspoons baking powder
1 teaspoon baking soda
1½ teaspoons cinnamon
1¼ cups honey
¾ cup apple juice
⅓ cup canola oil
4 eggs
2 cups grated **carrots**
¾ cup chopped walnuts

In mixing bowl, blend wheat flour, oatmeal, baking powder, baking soda, cinnamon, honey, apple juice, oil, and eggs. Let oatmeal soak for few minutes. Beat mixture for several minutes until smooth. Add carrots and walnuts. Spread into greased 9x13-inch pan. Bake at 325 degrees for 55 minutes. Cool. Frost with cream cheese frosting.

Mary Yoder, Mount Gilead, OH

Corn

Corn Chowder

5 slices bacon, chopped
1 medium onion, chopped
2 diced potatoes
½ cup water
2 cups milk
2 cups corn
1 teaspoon salt
Dash pepper

In saucepan or skillet, brown bacon and onion. Add potatoes and water, cooking until potatoes are tender. Add milk, corn, salt, and pepper.

Malinda Gingerich, Hartford, KS

Golden Corn Fritters

2 eggs, slightly beaten
¾ cup milk
1¼ cups flour
1¼ teaspoons baking powder
1 teaspoon salt
1 pound whole kernel corn, drained
Coconut oil for frying

In bowl, combine eggs and milk. In another bowl, sift together flour, baking powder, and salt. Beat into egg mixture. Add corn and mix well. Drop by teaspoon into hot (375 degrees) oil and fry until golden. Drain on paper towel. Serve with ketchup or other dipping sauce. Makes about 2 dozen fritters.

Mrs. Atlee (Clara) Yoder, Big Prairie, OH

Pickled Corncobs

Corncobs no longer than 4 inches
½ cup sugar
2 cups apple cider vinegar
1½ cups water
1 teaspoon kosher salt
1 teaspoon whole pickling spice

Pack corncobs into pint jars leaving ½-inch headspace. In saucepan, combine sugar, vinegar, water, and salt. Tie pickling spice into cheesecloth and add to saucepan. Bring mixture to boil for 5 minutes. Remove spice bundle. Ladle brine over corncobs to fill jars, leaving a ½-inch headspace. Cold pack in hot water bath for 15 minutes. Wait to eat after a week.

Grace Zimmerman, Shiloh, OH

Hominy

10 gallons water
8 gallons white or yellow shelled corn
32 ounces lye
Salt

In large cast-iron kettle, bring water to boil. Add corn and bring to boiling point. Add lye. Cook 30 minutes or until black ends of corn come off when you stir a few kernels in dipper of cold water. Immediately remove from heat and start washing the kernels in cold water. Put kernels of corn back in cleaned kettle, cover with fresh water, and bring to boil. Boil and wash three times. We wash ours in the yard with a garden hose. Drain after last wash and pack into quart canning jars. To each jar, add 1 tablespoon of salt and fill with fresh water. Pressure can at 10 pounds pressure for 1 hour. This is a big batch that will usually make 100 quarts.

Hominy is good drained and fried with meat, as pizza topping, or just heated with butter and topped with cheese.

Jemima Girod, Salem, IN

Cucumbers

Cucumber Refresher

25 cups **cucumber** juice
20 cups sparkling water
10 cups lemonade
2½ cups lime juice

Make cucumber juice by blending cucumbers in blender and straining out pulp. To juice, add sparkling water, lemonade, and lime juice. Stir well. Serve over ice.

Mary Yoder, Mount Gilead, OH

Cucumber Dip

1 (8 ounce) package cream cheese, softened
½ cup sour cream
½ cup peeled and grated **cucumber**, drained
2 tablespoons chopped celery
1 tablespoon chopped onion
½ teaspoon lemon juice
½ teaspoon sugar

Put all ingredients in blender and process until smooth. Serve with cut vegetables or crackers.

Rachel Schwartz, Bryant, IN

Creamy Cucumber Salad

2 to 3 cups shredded **cucumbers**
½ cup chopped onion
1 cup sour cream
1 cup salad dressing or mayonnaise
⅓ cup evaporated cane sugar
1 teaspoon salt
1 teaspoon celery salt
2 tablespoons lemon juice

Mix all ingredients together, chill, and serve.

Susan L. Gingerich, Dalton, OH

Sara Yoder, Mt. Gilead, OH

Refrigerator Pickles

These are our favorite pickles and so easy to make.

6 cups sliced cucumbers
½ cup sliced onions
¼ cup sliced peppers
2 cups sugar
1 cup white vinegar
1 to 2 teaspoons salt
2 teaspoons celery seed or
  1 teaspoon celery salt

In bowl or large jar, place cucumbers, onions, and peppers. In another bowl, mix sugar, vinegar, salt, and celery seed. Pour over vegetables. Refrigerate for at least 24 hours before eating. These keep a long time.

Lori Miller, Middlefield, OH

Mrs. Levi (Elsie) Schlabach, Big Prairie, OH

Sun Pickles

Whole (5 inch) pickles or
  your size preference
1 tablespoon pickling spice
½ cup salt
1½ cups vinegar
7½ cups water
Garlic to taste
Dill to taste

Put all ingredients in gallon jar with lid and place in sun for 3 days. Rotate or shake occasionally. Refrigerate until crisp.

Eidith Eicher, Colon, MI

Sweet and Sour Dill Pickles

4 quarts sliced cucumbers
8 head dill
16 slices onion
4 cups vinegar
2 cups water
⅓ cup salt
4 cups sugar

Fill 4 quart or 8 pint jars with sliced cucumbers. Divide dill and onions equally between jars. In saucepan, combine vinegar, water, salt, and sugar. Bring to boil. Fill jars with syrup. Seal jars in hot water bath by covering jars in water and bringing water to boil for about 5 minutes.

Mrs. Mosie A. Glick, Kimbolton, OH

Bread and Butter Pickles

1 gallon firm cucumbers, sliced thin
1 quart onions, thinly sliced
½ cup salt
5 cups sugar
1½ teaspoons turmeric
2 teaspoons mustard seed
1 teaspoon celery seed
2 cups vinegar
2 cups water

In bowl, cover cucumbers and onions in salt. Let stand 3 hours, covered with heavy lid. Drain and place in stockpot. Add sugar, turmeric, mustard seed, celery seed, vinegar, and water. Heat to boiling point. Ladle into pint canning jars. Seal in hot water bath for 8 minutes.

Sadie Bender, Meyersdale, PA

I add 2 thin-sliced green peppers.

Clara Miller, Walhonding, OH

Lovina Weaver, Big Prairie, OH

Pickle Relish

1 gallon ground cucumbers
1 pint ground onion
¼ cup salt
6 cups sugar
3 cups vinegar
3 teaspoons mustard seed
3 teaspoons celery seed
2 teaspoons turmeric

In a bowl, combine cucumber, onion, and salt. Let sit for 2 hours. Drain. Place relish in stockpot with sugar, vinegar, mustard seed, celery seed, and turmeric and bring to boiling point. Ladle into jars. To seal, place in hot water bath for 8 minutes.

Maggie Bontrager, Sturgis, MI

Summertime Pickles

- 4 cups sugar
- 4 cups water
- 1 cup white vinegar
- 1 tablespoon salt
- Pickles or small cucumbers
- Onions
- Turmeric
- Alum

In saucepan combine sugar, water, vinegar, and salt. Bring to boil. Into quart jars, pack pickles. Add some onion to your preference. To each quart jar add 1 teaspoon turmeric and ¾ teaspoon alum. Fill jars with syrup. Cold pack for 5 minutes to seal.

Ada E. Zook, Dalton, OH

Cinnamon Pickles

- 8 pounds cucumbers, peeled, seeds removed, and cut into small sticks
- 2 cups pickling lime
- 2 gallons cold water
- 4 cups vinegar
- 4 cups water
- 2 tablespoons salt
- 8 cups sugar
- 6 cinnamon sticks
- 10 ounces cinnamon hearts candy
- Red food coloring (optional)

Place cucumbers in large non-metal container. Mix lime and cold water, pouring over cucumbers. Soak for 24 hours. Drain and rinse well. Cover with fresh water and let stand 2 hours. Meanwhile, in stockpot, prepare syrup by combining vinegar, water, salt, sugar, cinnamon sticks, cinnamon candy, and food coloring as desired. Bring to boil and simmer until cinnamon candy is fully dissolved. Drain cucumbers and pour syrup over them. Let set overnight. Next morning, simmer mixture for 40 minutes. Pack while hot into sterile canning jars and seal in hot water bath for 8 minutes.

Sadie Bender, Meyersdale, PA

Eggplant

Fried Eggplant

1 eggplant, peeled and sliced
1 egg, beaten
Saltine crackers, crushed fine
Coconut oil

Dip eggplant in egg then in crackers. Fry in hot coconut oil. Very good eaten on bread with butter or with tomato sandwich.

Mrs. Sheryl Byler, Vestaburg, MI

Eggplant Casserole

1½ cups cooked and mashed **eggplant**
3 cups breadcrumbs
1 teaspoon salt
Pinch pepper
1 cup milk
⅔ cup shredded cheese
3 tablespoons melted butter
3 eggs

Mix all ingredients together and put in greased casserole dish. Bake at 350 degrees for about 1 hour.

Moses and Leah Renno, Jackson, OH

Greens

Strawberry Spinach Salad

1 bag small leaf spinach
1 bag red romaine lettuce
1 red onion, sliced
½ quart strawberries, sliced
1 cup halved pecans toasted in 1 tablespoon butter and sprinkled with sugar
½ cup shredded Mozzarella cheese

In large bowl, toss all ingredients together.

Vinaigrette:

⅓ cup white vinegar
½ cup sugar
1 cup or less oil
1 teaspoon salt
1 teaspoon dry mustard
1½ teaspoons dried onion
1½ tablespoons poppyseeds
2 tablespoons raspberry syrup

Mix all ingredients well and drizzle over salad and toss to coat. Serve immediately.

Mary Alice Yoder, Middlebury, IN

Spinach Loaf

1 pound spinach, washed and chopped
4 eggs, beaten
2 tablespoons spelt flour
1 teaspoon salt
Shredded cheese

In bowl, mix spinach, eggs, flour, and salt, and pour into buttered loaf pan. Bake at 350 degrees for 45 minutes. Top with cheese and allow to melt in oven before serving. Optional: Add protein of cooked and crumbled bacon, beef, or sausage.

Esther Troyer, Walhonding, OH

Mushrooms

Marinated Mushrooms

1 pound fresh **mushrooms**
½ cup sliced green onion
¼ cup chopped red bell peppers
2 tablespoons minced fresh parsley
1 (8 ounce) bottle Italian dressing

In bowl, combine all ingredients and allow to marinate for several hours or overnight before serving.

Katie Esh, Charlotte Court House, VA

Cream of Mushroom Soup

This tastes as good as what you can buy, but is a lot less expensive.

6 cups chopped **mushrooms**
8 cups rich milk or half-and-half
8 teaspoons onion powder
8 tablespoons vegetable oil
1 teaspoon pepper
2 teaspoons salt
½ teaspoon sugar
16 tablespoons Perma Flo

In kettle, mix mushrooms, milk, onion powder, oil, pepper, salt, and sugar. Bring to a boil. Mix Perma Flo with a little additional milk to make a paste. Add to soup and cook until thick. Ladle into pint canning jars, leaving 1 inch headspace, and seal at 10 pounds pressure for 30 minutes.

Rebecca Mast, Elkhart Lake, WI

Mushroom and Green Bean Pie

3 cups sliced fresh **mushrooms**
4 tablespoons butter, divided
2½ cups chopped onions (or less)
6 cups cut fresh green beans (1-inch pieces)
2 teaspoons minced fresh thyme or ¾ teaspoon dried thyme
½ teaspoon salt
¼ teaspoon pepper
1 (8 ounces) package cream cheese, cubed
½ cup milk

In large skillet, sauté mushrooms in 1 tablespoon butter until tender. Drain and set aside. In the same skillet, sauté onions and beans in remaining butter for 18 to 20 minutes until beans are crisp-tender. Add thyme, salt, pepper, cream cheese, and milk. Cook and stir until cheese is melted. Remove from heat; set aside.

Crust:

2½ cups flour
2 teaspoons baking powder
1 teaspoon dill weed
¼ teaspoon salt
1 cup cold butter
1 cup sour cream
1 egg
1 tablespoon whipping cream

In bowl, combine the flour, baking powder, dill weed, and salt. Cut in butter until mixture resembles coarse crumbs. Stir in sour cream to form soft dough. Divide dough in half on well-floured surface. Roll out one portion of dough to fit deep-dish 9-inch pie plate. Trim dough even with edge of plate. Pour green bean mixture into crust. Roll out remaining dough and slice strips to make lattice top crust. Trim dough and seal edges. In small bowl, beat egg then mix with whipping cream. Brush over crust. Bake at 400 degrees for 25 to 35 minutes or until golden brown.

Mrs. Amos Eicher, Monroe, IN

Onions

Onion Petals

Onions
Flour
1 egg
½ cup milk
3 cups Ritz cracker crumbs
2 cups flour
1½ teaspoons paprika
1 teaspoon pepper
3 tablespoons seasoned salt
1 tablespoon sugar
2 teaspoons Accent (optional)
1 tablespoon salt
2 teaspoons garlic salt
1½ tablespoons chicken base

Cut onions into petals or slices and sprinkle with flour. In bowl, beat together egg and milk. In another bowl, combine cracker crumbs, flour, paprika, pepper, seasoned salt, sugar, accent, salt, garlic salt, and chicken base. Dip onions in egg mixture then roll in dry mixture. Deep fry in oil or lard.

Dipping Sauce:

½ cup mayonnaise
2 tablespoons horseradish sauce
2 teaspoons ketchup
¼ teaspoon salt
⅛ teaspoon oregano
Dash pepper
Dash cayenne pepper

In bowl, blend all ingredients together.

Joann Miller, Fredericktown, OH

Onion Rings

These are a favorite in our house.

½ cup flour
1 tablespoon baking powder
1 teaspoon salt
½ teaspoon seasoned salt
1 egg, slightly beaten
¾ cup milk
1 tablespoon vegetable oil
2 large onions
Cooking oil

In bowl, combine flour, baking powder, salt, and seasoned salt. In another bowl, beat egg, milk, and oil. Stir flour mixture into egg mixture. Peel and slice onions fairly thick (at least ¼-inch slices), separating rings. Heat deep fryer with oil to 375 degrees. Dip rings of onion in batter one at a time and fry until golden brown. Flip and fry on other side. Place onion rings on paper-towel-lined platter.

Martha Beachy, Butler, OH

Onion Patties

¾ cup flour
1 tablespoon sugar
1 tablespoon cornmeal
2 teaspoons baking powder
1 teaspoon salt
¾ cup milk
2½ cups finely chopped **onion**

In bowl, mix flour, sugar, cornmeal, baking powder, and salt. Add milk. Batter should be fairly thick. Add onions and mix thoroughly. Heat a good coating of oil in skillet. Drop batter by spoonful into hot oil to fry. Flatten slightly when you turn patties. Fry until golden brown.

Mrs. Albert L. Yoder, Stanwood, MI

Onion Pie

30 small crackers, crushed
½ cup melted butter
3 cups sliced **onions**
¼ cup butter
½ pound shredded cheese
1½ cups milk, scalded
3 eggs, beaten
1 teaspoon salt
½ teaspoon pepper

In bowl, mix cracker crumbs with ½ cup melted butter and press into greased, shallow, 2-quart baking dish. In skillet, sauté onions in butter. Pour over crackers. Sprinkle with cheese. In saucepan, scald the milk then add eggs, salt, and pepper. Pour over cheese. Bake at 350 degrees for 30 minutes or until set like custard.

Mrs. Leander Miller, Vestaburg, MI

Peas

Shortcut Peas

Instead of shelling **peas**, wash pods and discard any spoilage. Place them in kettle of boiling water. As pods cook, they open. Pods float to top while peas sink to bottom. Peas cooked in this manner have fine flavor.

Barbara Stutzman, Apple Creek, OH

Spring Peas and Potatoes

Scrub and peel new potatoes. Cook until tender. Place in casserole dish. Top potatoes with thin layer of cooked fresh **peas**. Cover with generous amount of white sauce. If desired, sprinkle with cheddar cheese. Since all ingredients are hot, bake at 350 degrees just until cheese is melted.

White Sauce:

- 3 tablespoons butter
- 2 tablespoons flour
- 1 cup milk
- Salt and pepper to taste

In saucepan, melt butter and add flour, stirring until light brown. Add milk, stirring until thickened. Season to taste. Adjust amount to the size of your casserole.

Mrs. Rebecca Herschberger, Bear Lake, MI

Peppers

Jalapeño Poppers

Jalapeño or banana peppers
¼ cup cream cheese
½ cup shredded cheese
Bacon
Seasoned salt

Slice pepper tops off and remove seeds. In bowl, blend cream cheese and shredded cheese. Fill peppers with cheese mixture. Wrap slice of bacon around pepper, using toothpick to secure both ends. Season bacon with seasoned salt to taste. Put on hot grill, turning until bacon is crispy.

Tena Byler, Wilcox, PA

Jalapeño Popper Balls

3 jalapeño peppers, finely chopped
4 ounces cream cheese
4 ounces shredded Mozzarella cheese
4 ounces shredded cheddar cheese
½ cup flour
½ teaspoon paprika
½ teaspoon garlic powder
½ teaspoon onion powder
1 to 2 beaten eggs
Plain breadcrumbs

In bowl, mix pepper, cream cheese, Mozzarella cheese, and cheddar cheese. Make balls with cookie scoop and place on baking sheet. Freeze for 30 minutes. In another bowl, mix flour, paprika, garlic powder, and onion powder. Roll frozen balls into mixture then dip into beaten egg then into breadcrumbs. Deep fry in oil at 350 degrees until lightly browned.

Linda Fisher, Ronks, PA

Canned BBQ Hot Pepper Rings

These are very good on sandwiches and meatloaf.

32 ounces spaghetti sauce
½ cup barbecue sauce
6 ounces ketchup
2 cups sugar
1 cup vegetable oil
1 cup vinegar
1 tablespoon salt
½ to ¾ gallon sliced **hot peppers** (with or without seeds)

In saucepan, combine spaghetti sauce, barbecue sauce, ketchup, sugar, oil, vinegar, and salt. Boil for 10 to 15 minutes. Add peppers and cook 15 minutes more. Ladle into pint canning jars and seal with 2-part lids. Submerge into canner of hot water and bring to boiling point. Turn off heat. Remove from water when it has cooled. Yields 7 pints.

Barbara A. Swartzentruber, Dalton, OH

Hot Pepper Butter

42 **hot peppers**
1 pint mustard
1 quart vinegar
6 cups sugar
1 tablespoon salt
1 cup flour
1½ cups water

Chop hot peppers. In saucepan, mix peppers with mustard, vinegar, sugar, and salt. Heat. In bowl, make paste with flour and water. Add to peppers and bring to boil. Pour into pint canning jars and cold pack for 15 minutes. Good spread on sandwiches.

Amanda Miller, Middlefield, OH

Stuffed Peppers

Butter
1 onion, diced
2 pounds ground beef
Salt and pepper to taste
1 cup rice
2 cups water
Pinch salt
4 ounces cream cheese
1 cup sour cream
1 cup shredded Velveeta cheese
1 cup pizza sauce
2 tablespoons taco seasoning
8 red or green **bell peppers**
Mozzarella cheese

In skillet, brown butter then sauté onion. Add beef and season with salt and pepper, cooking until browned. In saucepan, cook rice in 2 cups water with pinch of salt. In large bowl, blend cream cheese, sour cream, Velveeta cheese, pizza sauce, and taco seasoning. Add beef and rice. Cut peppers in half and remove seeds. Fill peppers with beef mixture and place in casserole dish. If there is mixture leftover, place in dish between peppers. (Or, we have simply chopped up the peppers and added it to the mix.) Cover and bake at 350 degrees for 45 minutes. Uncover and top with Mozzarella cheese. Bake at 350 degrees for 10 to 15 minutes.

Mary Gingerich, Dalton, OH

Sweet Peppers to Can

These are crisp and nice to put on pizza or to use in salads.

- Red or green bell peppers
- 1 quart apple cider vinegar
- 1 pint water
- 1 cup organic raw cane sugar
- 1½ teaspoons salt
- Oil

Cut peppers in pieces and pack into canning jars. In saucepan, combine vinegar, water, sugar, and salt and boil for few minutes. Set canning jars in pan of hot water to warm. To each jar, add oil (1 tablespoon per quart; 1½ teaspoons per pint). Ladle boiling vinegar mixture into each jar. Place lids and rings on immediately. Do not pressure cook or hot water bath.

Simon and Ida Miller, Clark, MO

Pepper Mix

- 8 quarts mild hot peppers, cut into rings
- 4 quarts sweet peppers, cut into strips
- 2 cans black olives, drained
- 2 cups olive oil
- 5 cups white vinegar
- 5 cups sugar
- 1 cup salt
- 2½ to 3 tablespoons minced garlic
- ¼ cup fresh oregano

In large container, combine hot peppers, sweet peppers, and olives. In large bowl, mix olive oil, vinegar, sugar, salt, garlic, and oregano. Pour over peppers and set aside to marinate for 24 hours. Divide mixture into jars with tight lids. No need to seal or heat. Should keep for up to a year in refrigerator or cold storage. You can reduce heat by replacing some hot pepper with sweet pepper, cauliflower, carrots, or onion.

Fannie M. Peachey, Spring Run, PA

Potatoes

Potato Wedge Rolls

1 package yeast
½ cup warm water
1 cup milk
½ cup sugar
¾ cup shortening
2 teaspoons salt
2 eggs, beaten
1¼ cups mashed **potatoes,** pumpkin, or sweet potatoes
8 to 8½ cups flour

In small bowl, dissolve yeast in warm water. In mixing bowl, combine milk, sugar, shortening, salt, eggs, and potatoes until smooth. Add yeast. Add enough flour to be smooth but not dry. Mix and let set to rise. Punch down and let rise 1 hour. Divide dough into 3 or 4 portions. Roll out into circle and cut into 12 wedges with pizza cutter. Roll up each wedge, starting at broad end. Repeat with each portion. Place on greased baking sheets. Let rise. Bake at 400 degrees for 15 minutes.

Anna M. Weaver, Mertztown, PA

Sweet Potato Biscuits

2¼ cups flour
2 teaspoons baking powder
¾ cup sugar
1¼ teaspoons salt
5 tablespoons butter
2 cups cooked and mashed **sweet potatoes**

In mixing bowl, mix flour, baking powder, sugar, salt, and butter. Stir in sweet potatoes. Drop by spoonful onto baking sheet or roll dough out and cut in circles. Bake at 450 degrees for 20 minutes.

Jolene Bontrager, Nappanee, IN

Potato Salad

8 cups cubed or grated potatoes or macaroni
1½ cups diced celery
1½ cups grated carrots
½ cup diced onion
6 hard-boiled eggs, diced
Cheese, cubed (optional)
Salt to taste
3 cups salad dressing or Miracle Whip
1½ cups sugar
¼ cup prepared mustard
¼ cup vinegar

Cook potatoes before cubing or grating (or cook macaroni until tender). Mix with celery, carrots, onion, eggs, and cheese. In bowl, mix salad dressing, sugar, mustard, and vinegar. Mix with vegetables. Chill before serving.

Mrs. Albert L. Yoder, Stanwood, MI

Hashbrowns

1 cup flour
⅓ cup cornmeal
3 teaspoons salt
1 teaspoon baking powder
5 cups shredded **potatoes**
1 medium onion, chopped
⅓ cup oil
2 eggs
Cooking oil

Mix all ingredients together. In skillet, heat cooking oil and drop mixture by spoonful into hot oil, frying on both sides.

Alma Coblentz, Ashland, OH

Parsley Potatoes

1 cup butter
3 teaspoons salt
1 teaspoon seasoned salt
1 teaspoon garlic salt
2 tablespoons parsley
½ teaspoon pepper
½ teaspoon paprika
4 quarts diced **potatoes**

In saucepan, melt butter and add salt, seasoned salt, garlic salt, parsley, pepper, and paprika. Pour over potatoes and stir to coat well. Place potatoes in roasting pan. Bake at 350 degrees for 1½ hours.

Joann Miller, Fredericktown, OH

Baked Potato Slices

Medium-sized **potatoes**
Butter
Seasoned salt
Garlic salt
Parsley

Peel potatoes and cut into 1-inch slices lengthwise. Melt some butter and spread over bottom of glass casserole dish. Layer potatoes into dish and pour more butter over the potatoes. Sprinkle with seasoned salt, garlic salt, and parsley. Bake uncovered at 350 degrees for 45 to 60 minutes until soft and crisp.

Mrs. Albert L. Yoder, Stanwood, MI

Rosemary Roasted Potatoes

3 pounds **potatoes**
⅓ cup olive oil
1 tablespoon fresh rosemary
1 tablespoon minced chives
1 teaspoon salt
1 teaspoon pepper
¼ teaspoon garlic powder
Sour cream

Cut potatoes into quarters (yields about 8 cups). In small bowl, mix oil, rosemary, chives, salt, pepper, and garlic powder. In large bowl, toss oil mixture over potatoes. Spread on large baking sheet lined with parchment paper. Bake at 425 degrees for 35 minutes. Serve with sour cream.

Saloma Zook, Fredericksburg, OH

Dutch Potato Soup

2 cups diced potatoes
½ cup diced onion
3 cups water
1 teaspoon salt
1 cup chopped celery
½ cup grated carrot
1 quart milk
2 tablespoons butter
3 hard-boiled eggs, chopped
1 tablespoon parsley

In saucepan, bring potatoes, onion, water, and salt to boil. Simmer briefly. Add celery and carrot when potatoes are partially cooked. In separate saucepan, heat milk. When potatoes are soft, add heated milk. Stir in butter, eggs, and parsley just before serving.

Malinda Gingerich, Hartford, KS

Bacon Cheddar Potato Skins

4 large baking **potatoes**, baked
3 tablespoons oil
1 tablespoon grated Parmesan cheese
½ teaspoon salt
¼ teaspoon garlic powder
¼ teaspoon paprika
⅛ teaspoon pepper
8 strips bacon, cooked and crumbled
1½ cups shredded cheddar cheese
½ cup sour cream
4 green onions, sliced

Cut potatoes in half lengthwise. Scoop out pulp, leaving ¼-inch shell. (Save potato pulp for another use.) Place potato skins on greased baking sheet. In bowl, combine oil, Parmesan cheese, salt, garlic powder, paprika, and pepper. Brush over both sides of skins. Bake at 475 degrees for 5 to 7 minutes until crisp. Sprinkle insides of skins with bacon and cheese. Bake about 2 minutes until cheese is melted. Serve immediately with sour cream and green onion.

Lucinda Eicher, Monroe, IN

German Pizza

2 tablespoons butter
6 medium **potatoes**, shredded
Salt and pepper to taste
1 pound ground beef or sausage, browned
½ cup chopped green pepper
½ cup chopped onion
3 eggs, beaten
⅓ cup milk
Cheese, shredded

Melt butter in frying pan. Add potatoes, salt, and pepper. Fry until potatoes are almost soft. Layer with hamburger, green pepper, and onions. In bowl, mix eggs with milk and pour over all. Simmer until set. Top with cheese and let melt.

Lovina Weaver, Big Prairie, OH

Baked Potato Wedges

6 large potatoes
½ cup flour
1 teaspoon salt
¼ teaspoon pepper
¼ cup cheddar cheese powder or Parmesan cheese
½ teaspoon garlic powder
⅓ cup butter

Peel and slice potatoes into wedges. Rinse in cold water and drain. In plastic bag or bowl with tight lid, combine flour, salt, pepper, cheese powder, and garlic powder. While potatoes are still moist, place them in mixture and shake to coat well. In 9x13-inch pan, melt butter in 425-degree oven. Place potatoes in pan and bake at 425 degrees for 50 to 60 minutes, turning once during baking. Serve with ketchup or sour cream. Note: Fresh-from-the-garden potatoes may not need to be peeled.

Ruby Ann Hochstettler, New Holstein, WI

Potato Chips

2 gallons water
1 tablespoon alum
Potatoes, raw and thinly sliced
Oil for frying

Soak potatoes in water and alum for at least 1 hour. Drain well and fry in hot oil of your choice at 400 degrees until chips are crisp. Drain and season as desired.

Annie Peachy, Letart, WV

Fat Fellows

6 large potatoes
½ cup butter
½ cup milk
½ cup sour cream
2 teaspoons salt
Dash pepper
Cheese
Bacon bits

Scrub potatoes and wrap in foil. Bake at 450 degrees for 45 to 60 minutes until done. When cool, cut in half and scoop out insides, leaving shell intact. In mixing bowl, whip potatoes then mix in butter, milk, sour cream, salt, and pepper. Beat until smooth. Stuff potato mixture into potato shells. Sprinkle with cheese and bacon bits. Bake at 425 degrees for 20 minutes.

Sara Yoder, Mt. Gilead, OH

Battered Fries

⅔ cup milk
⅓ cup flour
½ cup runion breading mix
¾ teaspoon baking powder
1 teaspoon salt
5 to 6 potatoes

In bowl, mix milk, flour, breading mix, baking powder, and salt. Cut potatoes a little wider than regular fries. Dry them on paper towel and dip into batter. Deep fry in oil at 325 degrees until golden and soft. Delicious served with ranch dressing.

Maria Zook, Dalton, OH

Crispy Baked Sweet Potato Fries

Healthy and delicious!

2 sweet potatoes, cut into thin sticks
1 egg white (optional)
2 tablespoons olive oil
Salt to taste
Garlic powder to taste
Pepper to taste

Preheat oven to 450 degrees and place baking sheet in it to warm for 5 to 10 minutes. This is necessary to get potatoes crispy. In bowl, whisk egg white, oil, salt, garlic powder, and pepper. Add sweet potatoes and mix well to coat. Brush piece of parchment paper lightly with olive oil and place on hot baking sheet. Place sweet potatoes on paper. Bake at 450 degrees for 20 minutes, flipping halfway.

Mrs. Levi (Elsie) Schlabach, Big Prairie, OH

Honey-Glazed Sweet Potatoes

- 2 pounds sweet potatoes
- 6 tablespoons butter, melted
- 1 teaspoon fresh lemon juice
- 3 tablespoons honey
- Salt and pepper to taste

Cut sweet potatoes into ½- to ¾-inch squares. Mix with butter, lemon juice, honey, salt, and pepper. Bake at 425 degrees for 20 to 30 minutes or until potatoes are soft.

Lena Miller, Gallipolis, OH

Sara Yoder, Mt. Gilead, OH

Sweet Potato Casserole

- 4 cups cooked and mashed sweet potatoes
- ½ cup sugar
- 2 eggs
- ½ teaspoon salt
- 7 tablespoons melted butter, divided
- ½ cup milk
- ½ teaspoon vanilla
- ½ cup brown sugar
- ⅓ cup flour
- ½ cup chopped pecans

In bowl, combine sweet potatoes, sugar, eggs, salt, 4 tablespoons melted butter, milk, and vanilla. Mix until smooth. Put in 9x13-inch baking pan. In bowl, blend brown sugar, flour, 3 tablespoons melted butter, and pecans. Sprinkle on top of casserole. Bake at 350 degrees for 30 minutes until lightly browned.

Marilyn Schwartz, Monroe, IN

Radishes

Radish Dip

- 1 (8 ounce) package cream cheese, softened
- ½ cup sour cream
- ½ teaspoon sugar
- 2 cups diced **radish** (or adjust to taste)

Put all ingredients in blender and process until smooth and creamy. Serve with club crackers or other favorite crackers.

Ruth Miller, Fredericksburg, OH

Pickled Daikon and Carrots

- 1 medium daikon **radish**, peeled and julienned
- 1 cup julienned carrots
- 2 jalapeño peppers, seeded and sliced
- ¾ cup water
- ¾ cup white vinegar
- ⅓ cup sugar
- 1 teaspoon kosher salt
- 2 drops liquid smoke (optional)

In large bowl, combine radish, carrots, and peppers. In saucepan, bring water, vinegar, sugar, salt, and liquid smoke to boil. Simmer until sugar dissolves. Pour mixture over vegetables ensuring all vegetables are submerged. Cool. Refrigerate with cover at least 1 hour before serving. To store, transfer to jars and cover tightly. Keeps in refrigerator at least 2 weeks. Tasty condiment on burger or sandwich.

Mrs. Amos Eicher, Monroe, IN

Rhubarb

Rhubarb Punch

12 cups chopped **rhubarb**
8 cups water
4 cups sugar
1 can frozen orange juice concentrate

In saucepan, cook rhubarb in water until soft. Strain liquid through sieve until all rhubarb juice is out. Add sugar and orange juice to rhubarb juice. Add water to equal 3 gallons.

Henry and Lovina Shetler, Pierpont, OH

Rhubarb Juice to Can

8 pounds **rhubarb, chopped**
10 quarts water
2 boxes strawberry gelatin
2 cups pineapple juice
5 cups sugar
¼ cup lemon juice

In stockpot, cook rhubarb in water until soft. Drain and retain juice. To hot juice, add gelatin, pineapple juice, sugar, and lemon juice. Pour into 12 to 13 quart jars. Cold pack for 10 minutes to seal.

To serve, dilute juice with some lemon-lime soda and serve over ice.

Rebecca Byler, Spartansburg, PA

Rhubarb Bread

1½ cups brown sugar
⅓ cup oil
1 egg, beaten
1 teaspoon baking soda
1 teaspoon salt
1 teaspoon vanilla
1 cup sour milk
2½ cups flour
1½ cups diced **rhubarb**
½ cup chopped nuts
1 tablespoon butter
½ cup brown sugar

In mixing bowl, blend 1½ cups brown sugar and oil. Mix in egg. Add baking soda, salt, vanilla, sour milk, and flour. Fold in rhubarb and nuts. Pour into 2 greased loaf pans. In bowl, mix butter and ½ cup brown sugar, sprinkling on top of loaves. Bake at 325 degrees for 1½ hours.

Malinda Gingerich, Hartford, KS

Rhubarb Sauce

12 cups chopped **rhubarb**
9 cups water
4 cups cane sugar
1½ cups raspberry gelatin
1¼ cups Perma Flo or ThermFlo
2½ cups water

In stockpot, simmer rhubarb, 9 cups water, and sugar together until rhubarb is soft. Stir in raspberry gelatin. In bowl, mix Perma Flo with 2½ cups water. Add to rhubarb. Bring to boil. Ladle into canning jars. If you bring it to boil and immediately put it into hot jars with hot lids, it should seal. You can also seal in water bath.

Anna Mae Mullet, Bremen, IN

Rhubarb Crunch

1 cup sugar
1 cup water
2 tablespoons cornstarch
2 tablespoons strawberry jam
1 teaspoon vanilla
4 cups chopped **rhubarb**
1 cup unbleached flour
1 cup rolled oats
1 cup brown sugar
½ cup melted butter
1 teaspoon cinnamon

In saucepan, whisk together sugar, water, and cornstarch, cooking until thickened. Remove from heat and add strawberry jam and vanilla. Mix in rhubarb. In mixing bowl, combine flour, oats, brown sugar, butter, and cinnamon until crumbs form. Lightly press half of crumb mixture in 9x9-inch pan. Top with rhubarb mixture. Sprinkle with remaining crumb mixture. Bake at 350 degrees for 45 minutes. Delicious served warm with vanilla ice cream.

Saloma Zook, Fredericksburg, OH

Rhubarb Cream Pie

2 cups diced **rhubarb**
1 unbaked pie shell
2 tablespoons strawberry gelatin
1 egg
1 cup sugar
2 tablespoons flour
2 cups cream
¼ teaspoon salt
½ teaspoon vanilla

Place rhubarb in pie shell and sprinkle with gelatin. In bowl, beat egg, adding sugar, flour, cream, salt, and vanilla. Pour over rhubarb. Bake at 350 degrees for about an hour until custard is set but does not boil. Note: Peaches and peach gelatin can be substituted for rhubarb and strawberry gelatin.

Rachel Stutzman, Dalton, OH

"Go Anywhere" Rhubarb Squares

Crust:

2 cups flour
⅔ cup powdered sugar
⅔ cup butter

Mix and pat into greased jelly roll pan. Bake at 350 degrees for 12 minutes.

Filling:

½ cup flour
2 cups sugar
2 teaspoons vanilla
4 eggs
6 cup finely chopped **rhubarb**

In large bowl, blend flour, sugar, vanilla, and eggs. Fold in rhubarb until well coated. Pour over hot crust and bake at 325 degrees for 30 to 35 minutes. Cool completely then refrigerate to chill before cutting.

Mrs. Chester (Rose) Miller, Centerville, PA

Rhubarb Jam

5 cups diced rhubarb
4 cups sugar
1 (3 ounce) package cherry, raspberry, or strawberry gelatin

In kettle, mix rhubarb and sugar, letting it set overnight. The next morning, bring rhubarb to boil for 5 minutes, stirring constantly. Remove from heat and stir in gelatin. Ladle into pint jars and seal in hot water bath for 5 minutes.

Ruben and Ruth Schwartz, Connersville, IN
Mrs. William A. Hershberger, Poland, NY

Squash

Pumpkin Pie Smoothie

15 ounces **pumpkin** puree
1 teaspoon pumpkin pie spice
1 cup French vanilla creamer
1 cup milk
10 ice cubes
2 tablespoons brown sugar

Combine all ingredients in blender and blend until smooth.

Amanda Miller, Middlefield, OH

Butternut Squash Buns

2 tablespoons plus 1 teaspoon yeast
¾ teaspoon sugar
½ cup warm water
2 cups warm milk
2 teaspoons salt
¼ cup butter, softened
1 cup sugar
2 cups mashed **butternut squash**
10 to 11½ cups flour

In mixing bowl, dissolve yeast and ¾ teaspoon sugar in warm water. Let stand 5 minutes. Add warm milk, salt, butter, 1 cup sugar, and squash, mixing until smooth. Add 4 cups flour. Beat until smooth. Stir in enough flour to form dough and knead until smooth. Place dough in greased bowl, cover and let rise until doubled. Punch down and divide dough into 40 to 48 pieces and form loose balls. Place in greased pans. Cover and let rise until doubled. Bake at 400 degrees for 10 to 15 minutes. The recipe can be halved.

Lorina Miller, Mechanicstown, OH

Squash Casserole

- 2 cups cooked and mashed butternut squash
- ¾ cup cooked meat of choice
- 2 eggs
- 3 tablespoons melted butter
- 1 teaspoon salt
- ½ teaspoon pepper
- ¾ cup onions
- 1 cup shredded cheese
- 1 cup milk
- 2 cups crackers or breadcrumbs

Mix all ingredients together and place in casserole dish. Bake at 375 degrees for 40 minutes.

Leona Bontrager, Nappanee, IN

Zucchini Sandwich

One of our summertime favorites.

- 3 to 4 zucchini, chunked
- 1 pound ground beef or sausage
- 1 onion, sliced
- Salt to taste

In skillet, brown beef. When almost done, place zucchini and onion on top, cover and let steam until vegetables are soft. We usually eat this with bread and jelly. You can put cheese on top.

Sharon Rose Schmucker, Mayslick, KY

Zucchini Fries

- ½ cup finely crushed crackers
- ¼ cup Parmesan cheese
- 2 medium zucchini
- 1 egg, beaten
- Marinara sauce or ranch dressing

In bowl, mix crackers and cheese. Cut zucchini into short strips. Dip strips into egg then into crumb mixture. Place in single layer on greased baking sheet. Bake at 425 degrees for 20 minutes or until crispy, turning once. Serve with marinara sauce or ranch dressing.

Mrs. David A. Yoder, Millersburg, OH

Zucchini Fritters

2 cups grated zucchini
1½ cups flour
½ teaspoon salt
1½ teaspoons baking powder
2 ounces ranch powder or sour cream and onion powder
½ cup milk
1 egg, beaten
Oil

Mix zucchini, flour, salt, baking powder, ranch powder, and milk. Add beaten egg. More flour may be needed to make a thick, sticky batter. Heat 2 inches of oil in skillet and drop batter by spoonful into hot oil. Fry until golden brown on all sides. Eat warm with cheese sauce or ranch dressing. You can customize by adding chopped onions, diced green peppers, parsley, shredded carrots, or other things as desired.

Emma Kurtz, Smicksburg, PA

Fried Yellow Squash

¼ cup butter
2 medium yellow squash
Salt
Garlic powder
Onion powder
Black pepper

Melt butter in frying pan while chopping squash into ⅜-inch cubes. Add cubes to pan and sprinkle with salt, garlic powder, onion powder, and pepper. Stir-fry 10 minutes or until squash is tender and browning.

Note: This is meant to be a side dish, but I love to have it for breakfast or lunch with eggs cracked over top when squash is almost done. Yummy to leave egg yolks runny.

Esther Troyer, Walhonding, OH

Katie's Zucchini Patties

2 medium **zucchini**, grated
1 cup flour
1½ cups rolled oats
3 eggs
Salt and pepper to taste

Mix all together. Form patties and fry in greased skillet until firm and lightly brown on both sides.

Katie Swartzentruber, Newcomerstown, OH

Meat Lovers Zucchini Pizza

A delicious family favorite.

4 cups grated **zucchini**
2 eggs, slightly beaten
3 tablespoons Bisquick baking mix
1 teaspoon salt
1 cup shredded Mozzarella cheese, divided
1 cup shredded cheddar cheese, divided
Bacon, fried and crumbled
Ham, chopped
Smoky links
Pepperoni

In bowl, mix zucchini, eggs, Bisquick, salt, ½ cup Mozzarella cheese, and ½ cup cheddar cheese. Press into 9x11-inch pan. Bake at 400 degrees for 15 to 20 minutes until set. Top with ½ cup Mozzarella cheese, and ½ cup cheddar cheese, bacon, ham, smoky links, and pepperoni. Bake until cheese is melted.

Rebecca Herschberger, Bear Lake, MI

Zucchini Pizza Boats

This is a fun meal for children. Pizza with a bowl that they can eat. Great way to get them to eat zucchini.

Zucchini, sliced lengthwise
Sausage, uncooked
Pizza sauce
Pepperoni, slices
Cheese, shredded

Scoop seeds out of zucchini and stuff cavity with sausage. Put in single layer in cake pan. Add small amount of water (⅛ cup) in bottom of the pan. Cover with foil and bake at 375 degrees for 45 to 60 minutes until sausage is done and zucchini is tender but not mushy. Drain off liquid from pan. Pour pizza sauce over top. Put pepperoni on boats and sprinkle with cheese. Return to oven and bake until sauce is bubbly and cheese is melted.

Sarah Byler, Knox, PA

Zucchini Hash

2 tablespoons butter
1 medium **zucchini**, grated
1 pound ground beef or sausage
4 eggs, beaten
Salt and pepper to taste
Cheese, shredded

In skillet, melt butter and stir-fry zucchini until tender and juice is mostly gone. Add meat. Fry until slightly browned. Add eggs and season with salt and pepper. Stir until eggs are set. Put cheese on top and let melt through. Delicious served on buns or with fresh tomatoes.

Simon and Tillie Yoder, Hillsboro, WV

Zucchini Casserole

I make this every summer. It's delicious plus a great way to use up extra zucchini. You can even use those extra-large zucchini if you remove the seeds.

6 cups grated unpeeled **zucchini**
1 cup minced onion
Water
1 cup shredded carrots
1 (10 ounce) can cream of chicken soup
1 (8 ounce) carton sour cream
1 teaspoon salt
1½ cups cubed Velveeta cheese
⅛ teaspoon garlic salt
4 cups chopped cooked chicken or turkey
½ cup melted butter
1 box StoveTop dressing mix
2 cups shredded cheddar cheese

In large saucepan, combine zucchini and onion. Add water to cover and bring to boil for 5 minutes. Drain and cool. In bowl, combine carrots, soup, sour cream, salt, Velveeta cheese, and garlic salt. Add zucchini and chicken, mixing well. Spread into 9x13-inch baking pan. In bowl, blend melted butter into dressing mix. Spread on top of casserole and bake at 350 degrees for 30 to 60 minutes. In last 15 minutes, top with cheddar cheese.

Rebecca Herschberger, Bear Lake, MI

Summer Squash Casserole

6 cups sliced yellow squash
¼ cup chopped onion
¼ cup butter
1 can cream of mushroom soup
1 cup sour cream
8 slices toasted bread, cubed
½ cup melted butter
Chicken base
Garlic powder

In skillet, fry squash and onion in ¼ cup butter. In bowl, combine soup and sour cream. Add cooked squash. In another bowl, mix toasted bread cubes with butter and season to taste with chicken base and garlic powder. Layer half of bread cubes in roasting pan. Top with squash mixture then with remaining bread. Bake at 350 degrees for 30 to 40 minutes.

Mrs. Levi (Elsie) Schlabach, Big Prairie, OH

Zippy Zucchini Stew

1 to 2 tablespoons oil or butter
4 cups chopped onions
4 cups diced red and green peppers
6 cups diced zucchini
6 cups diced summer squash
12 cups tomato juice or diced tomatoes
6 cups cubed potatoes
4 cups diced carrots
1 teaspoon pepper
4 heaving teaspoons seasoned salt
1½ cups brown sugar

In large stockpot, heat oil and sauté onions, peppers, zucchini, and squash. In another pot, cook together tomato juice, potatoes, carrots, pepper, seasoned salt, and sugar until potatoes are tender. Add sautéed vegetables, mixing well. Divide into quart jars. Pressure can at 15 pounds for 15 minutes. When ready to eat, heat well and add cooked meat if desired. Yields 8 to 9 quarts.

Fannie L. Stuzman, West Salem, OH

Zucchini Chocolate Chip Loaves

3 cups flour
2 cups sugar
3 teaspoons cinnamon
1 teaspoon baking soda
½ teaspoon baking powder
½ teaspoon ground allspice
2 eggs
1 cup vegetable oil
3 teaspoons vanilla
2 cups grated **zucchini**
1 cup (6 ounces) chocolate chips
1 cup raisins (optional)

In large bowl, combine flour, sugar, cinnamon, baking soda, baking powder, and allspice. In small bowl, beat eggs, oil, and vanilla. Stir into dry mixture just until moistened. Fold in zucchini, chocolate chips, and raisins. Divide into 2 greased 4x8-inch loaf pans. Bake at 325 degrees for 60 to 75 minutes or until toothpick inserted near center comes out clean. Cool for 10 minutes before removing from pans to wire racks.

Anna M. Weaver, Mertztown, PA

Yellow Squash Pie

3½ cups chopped and cooked **yellow squash**
½ cup butter
2 eggs
2 tablespoons flour
1 cup sugar
1 teaspoon vanilla or lemon flavoring
1 deep-dish unbaked pie shell or 2 small pie shells

In blender, combine squash, butter, eggs, flour, sugar, and vanilla and blend until smooth. Pour into pie shell(s). Sprinkle with cinnamon and nutmeg. Bake at 375 degrees for 50 to 55 minutes. Cool and top with whipped topping to serve.

Danny and Ruth Detweiler, Tazewell, VA

Fudgy Zucchini Brownies

1½ cups grated zucchini
1 cup almond or peanut butter
½ cup honey
1 teaspoon baking soda
½ cup cocoa powder
¼ teaspoon salt
½ teaspoon vanilla
½ cup chocolate chips

In bowl, mix all ingredients together. Pour into greased 9x9-inch pan. Bake at 350 degrees for 35 to 40 minutes. Let cool. Refrigerate to harden before serving and serve cold.

Rachel Schwartz, Bryant, IN

Zucchini Cobbler

No one would ever guess that this dessert is made with zucchini. It tastes like apple crunch.

- 8 cups peeled, seeded, chopped zucchini
- ⅔ cup lemon juice
- 3 cups sugar, divided
- 2 teaspoons cinnamon, divided
- ½ teaspoon nutmeg (optional)
- 4 cups flour
- 1½ cups cold butter

In large saucepan over medium heat, cook and stir zucchini and lemon juice for 15 to 20 minutes or until tender. Add 1 cup sugar, 1 teaspoon cinnamon, and nutmeg. Simmer 1 minute then remove from heat. In mixing bowl, combine flour and 2 cups sugar. Cut in butter until mixture resembles coarse crumbs. Stir ½ cup of mixture into zucchini mixture. Press half of remaining crumb mixture into greased 10x15 baking sheet pan. Spread zucchini mixture on top. Crumble remaining crumbs on top. Sprinkle with 1 teaspoon cinnamon. Bake at 375 degrees for 35 to 45 minutes until golden brown and bubbly. Yields 16 to 20 servings.

Mrs. Ezra (Darla) Yoder, Homer, MI

Fresh Salsa

1 gallon chopped **tomatoes**
2 small onions, chopped
3 bell peppers, chopped
1 to 2 jalapeño peppers, diced (optional)
¼ cup fresh cilantro, chopped fine (optional)
1 teaspoon salt
¼ teaspoon pepper
14 teaspoons Accent

Mix all together and refrigerate a few hours. Serve with tortilla chips or corn chips.

Sylvia Schwartz, Geneva, IN

Fresh Tomato Sauce

This is a recipe a customer shared with me when we had a retail produce market.

3 tablespoons olive oil
¼ cup diced onion
2 tablespoons fresh minced garlic
½ cup water
32 ounces tomatoes, peeled and diced
1 tablespoon oregano
1 tablespoon salt
1 tablespoon pepper

In stockpot, heat olive oil and sauté onion for 5 minutes until opaque. Add garlic and cook 2 minutes. Add water, tomatoes, oregano, salt, and pepper. Bring to boil and simmer for 30 minutes. Serve over pasta or noodles. We like it served with rice or meat. It can be preserved by canning or freezing.

Anna M. Weaver, Mertztown, PA

Marinated Tomatoes

2 large **tomatoes**, chunked
1 bell pepper, chopped
1 onion, chopped
3 tablespoons vinegar
3 tablespoons olive oil
2 tablespoons sugar
1 teaspoon seasoned salt
½ teaspoon basil
½ teaspoon oregano
½ teaspoon garlic powder
¼ teaspoon pepper

Place tomatoes, green pepper, and onion in bowl. In separate small bowl, blend vinegar, oil, sugar, seasoned salt, basil, oregano, garlic powder, and pepper. Pour over tomatoes, stir, and refrigerate at least 2 hours before serving. Delicious with burgers.

Elsie Beiler, Fredericksburg, OH

Fried Green Tomatoes

Core green **tomatoes** and slice thin. Dip in beaten egg then roll in flour. Fry in hot butter. Season with salt and pepper as desired.

Moses and Leah Renno, Jackson, OH

Stuffed Cherry Tomatoes

11 ounces cream cheese, softened
2 tablespoons mayonnaise
1 (4 ounce) package ranch salad dressing mix
3 dozen **cherry tomatoes**

In mixing bowl, blend cream cheese, mayonnaise, and salad dressing mix until smooth. Slice thin slice off top of tomatoes and carefully remove insides. Invert tomatoes on paper towels to drain. Fill with cream cheese mixture.

Mary Yoder, Mount Gilead, OH

Easy Salad

Tomatoes
Onions
Green peppers
Pickles

Cut tomatoes, onions, green peppers, and pickles into small chunks. Place in bowl and mix. Spoon onto individual plates and top with ranch dressing. It is a simple and delicious salad.

We have a family of 10 children and a greenhouse where we plant around 400 tomato plants each year. We pick them, wash them, and take them to a produce auction to sell. We all love tomatoes, and we enjoy salads and sandwiches all through the summer.

Mrs. Ella Detweiler, Smicksburg, PA

Tomato Slice Salad

Core and peel **tomatoes**, slicing them ⅓-inch thick. Place single layer on individual plates. Spread 1 to 2 teaspoons mayonnaise or salad dressing on each slice. Chop equal parts green pepper and onions. Scatter over tomatoes. Grate some carrots and sprinkle over tomatoes. Top with shredded cheese. Sprinkle with little salt.

Moses and Leah Renno, Jackson, OH

Pizza Sauce

Our English neighbor lady gave this recipe to my mom around 30 years ago. She has used it ever since and it has become my favorite.

4 quarts chopped **tomatoes**, scaled and skinned
1 large onion, cut in chunks
1 red bell pepper, chopped
1 small hot pepper, diced
1 clove garlic, minced
¼ teaspoon basil
1 teaspoon oregano
2 teaspoons salt

In stockpot, combine all ingredients and bring to boil until it reaches desired thickness, 4 to 6 hours. Ladle into pint canning jars and process 30 minutes in hot water bath to seal. Yields 2 to 3 pints.

Anna M. Weaver, Mertztown, PA

Tomato Relish

1 cup chopped onion
2 quarts ripe **tomatoes**, peeled
2 medium green bell peppers, chopped
2 medium red bell peppers, chopped
2 cups chopped carrots
2 cups chopped apples
2¾ cups sugar
1½ cups vinegar
1 teaspoon cinnamon
1 tablespoon salt
½ scant teaspoon ground clove
2 teaspoons mustard seed

In small saucepan, cook onion in little water until tender. In stockpot, combine all remaining ingredients and bring to boil until vegetables are fairly tender. Add onions. Ladle into canning jars. Cold pack for 8 to 10 minutes to seal.

Lillian Yoder, Grantsville, MD

Tomatoes to Can

Peel **tomatoes**, chop, and pack into quart canning jars. Add 1 teaspoon salt to each quart. Cold pack for 20 minutes.

Margaret Wengerd, Bryant, IN

Six Day Ketchup

This is the only ketchup we use.

- ½ bushel **tomatoes**, sliced ½ inch thick
- Salt
- ¼ cup mixed pickling spice
- 3 medium onions, chopped
- ½ large pepper, chopped
- 3 tablespoons salt
- 5 to 6 cups sugar
- 1 cup vinegar
- 1 cup Perma Flo

Layer tomatoes in 5-gallon bucket. On each layer, sprinkle a handful of salt. Put flat plate on top of tomatoes and tie cloth over bucket. On next day, hold plate down and tip bucket to drain juices. Do this for 4 or 5 more days. Pick and toss top tomatoes that show any sign of decay or mold. Put remaining tomatoes through food mill then into stockpot. Tie pickling spice, onions, and peppers into cheesecloth bag and add to tomatoes. Simmer for at least 30 minutes. Remove bag and squeeze all juices from bag into tomatoes. Add 3 tablespoons salt, sugar, and vinegar. Bring to boil and thicken with Perma Flo. Ladle into canning jars and seal in water bath for 10 minutes.

Mrs. Roy (Ruby) Miller, Brinkhaven, OH

Our Pea Story

Every year as the earth warms in the spring, one of the first things to plant is peas. They do well in cooler weather, and a little snow here in central Ohio will do them no harm. For years we helped our mother plant the peas as close to St. Patrick's Day as possible. Now we have our own garden and still like to plant peas.

One year, Sarah went to the local hardware store that sells pea seeds in bulk. She bought a pound and brought them home. We made two rows, side by side, and planted those peas. Once the sprouts were starting to poke through the soil, we added panels of fence between the rows. The peas should eventually climb right up to the top. Each year we would always get many compliments on our nice rows of peas and would enjoy harvesting a good amount to eat and freeze.

But that year the peas were planted, the panels were set, but there were no peas. We decided the peas from the hardware store must have been old. So Sarah went back to the store and told them the peas had not grown. So they gave her another pound of seeds for free.

We planted the new seeds by the fence. This time we waited for two weeks, and again only a few plants came up. So Sarah took a trowel and dug along the row by the fence where the peas were planted, thinking she would find pea seeds. But instead, she found tunnels! A burrowing mole or vole had eaten both the first and second plantings of pea seeds.

That year no one complimented us on our nice rows of peas. Pride goeth before a fall!?!

After that last planting, it was too late in the season for a third planting. We ended up with only a few plants that the varmints missed, and we most certainly missed having lots of peas to eat that year.

Sarah went back to the hardware store and told them what happened, asking to pay for the seeds they had given her. They said, "No, just come back next year and buy your seeds here." Which, of course, we did.

A friend who heard our woes told us to use castor oil on the seeds, and that has been a success. Every year now when we open the pea seeds, we pour some castor oil on them. It doesn't take much, just a light coating. Then plant them. We don't know if the varmints get a belly ache or if the oil tastes awful, but after a few bites, they leave the rest alone.

For nearly thirty years, Mattie and Sarah grew up on the home farm in Holmes County. Now we have our own house and garden plus apple trees, grapes, strawberries, raspberries, and newly added blueberry bushes. There were ten children in the family, and growing up on the farm taught us many things. We learned how to plant and preserve food. We enjoy harvesting fresh fruits and vegetables. That is food at its very best!

MATTIE AND SARAH TROYER, Millersburg, OH

Farm Bounty

In this cookbook, we have highlighted many of things you can source for your table from local farms, including dairy, fruits, grains, nuts, seeds, meats, eggs, vegetables, and herbs. Here are a few other things that farmers produce.

- Flowers
- Honey
- Lard
- Maple Syrup
- Molasses
- Sorghum
- Teas
- Vinegar

Have fun exploring your local area and finding new sources of foods you can add to your family's table.

Index of Contributors

Index of Recipes by Category

Beverages

Breakfast

Breads

Salads and Dips

Side Dishes

Soups and Stews

Main Dishes

Desserts

Bars and Cookies

Cakes

Pies

Puddings and Other Desserts

Snacks

Dairy Products

Canned Goods and Preserves

Miscellaneous